Uncle Rob's Blog

Volume 1

Uncle Rob's Blog

Short Bible Messages That Are Sure to Brighten Your Day

Volume 1

Rob Perkins

© 2022 One Stone Press — All rights reserved.

All rights reserved. No part of this book may be reproduced in any form without written permission of the publisher.

Published by:
One Stone Press
979 Lovers Lane
Bowling Green, KY 42103

Printed in the United States of America

ISBN 13: 978-1-941422-71-7

For Julie

Foreword

Uncle Rob has a unique style of feeding and nurturing the flock of God over which he serves as an elder. At the close of each Lord's Day he communicates by email important information about the local church. He may pass along an elder's observation about attendance, member needs, or about the visitors who came that day to worship. His message may be an encouraging description of one of the members. In fact, he includes himself at times with self-deprecation because he too, as a humble child of God, faces life's trials. Altogether with this review each week every member of this congregation should be motivated to be "ready for every good work" (Titus 3:1).

Included in this weekly email is a scriptural lesson for edification of the reader. The book you hold in your hand is a collection of Uncle Rob's Blogs. Uncle Rob has a depth of spiritual knowledge that is made simple by his easy-to-read style. You will be surprised at the fresh insight and application of well-known Bible stories. I have read with regularity on Monday mornings this email sent out by Uncle Rob, and I have encouraged him to share them on a larger scale. This book is a result of many hours of work by Rob.

Dr. Robert W. Perkins, DVM works as a veterinarian at Tejas Veterinary Clinic in Corpus Christi, Texas. He has served as an elder of the Parkway Church of Christ since 1997. He and his wife, Julie, have two children: Walker (Wife, Jolen) and Lauren (Husband, Clark Underwood). They have been blessed with six grandchildren.

I am honored to recommend this series of blogs written by my friend and faithful elder of the Lord's church.

—Robert F. Harkrider

Preface

I started my Blog in 2009, I had been in the habit of sending an email to the congregation that occasionally included an article. My daughter (Lauren Perkins Underwood) suggested I write a blog so I did. The blog has evolved over the years and at this time contains nearly 800 articles.

I always sign off of my articles as "Uncle Rob." Several of the kids I know referred to me as "Uncle Rob" so I adopted that moniker.

The blog has also gone worldwide. There are over 83,000 views from almost every country in the world. I realize religious articles aren't for everyone but they are for some.

My stimulus for writing articles has been from my daily Bible reading, preparing for classes that I teach and sitting in classes that others teach as a student.

In addition, as you will see, I have used my work as a Veterinarian to illustrate biblical principles.

I have tried to organize and categorize these articles by subject but that's not the way they were written so please take that into account as you read. I noticed that as I cycled through the Bible in my daily Bible reading I would duplicate articles on the same subject but the content was significantly different as is reflected by my maturation as a Bible student.

My great friend and mentor Robert Harkrider is the one who encouraged me to publish the articles in book form.

I have served over 30 years as an Elder with David Smitherman and he has really shaped my thinking. Although we don't agree on every single thing I have great respect for him and have learned so much from him. I love the years I spent with him.

I could not have published this book without the help of folks like our current preacher, Marc Hinds, who has done the formatting. In addition, Warren and Paula Berkley along with Karen Stubbs have done the editing work for me. Who am I to have such great friends?

Of course, my wife Julie Perkins has been a great sounding board for me. You will see and understand her from some of these blog articles.

I sincerely hope that in some small way you might benefit from the way I view the scriptures. To God be the glory!

—Rob Perkins
November 2021

Contents

Foreword vii
Preface viii

Church

Building Us 2
Conflict In A Local Church And The Importance Of
    Leadership 3
Two Ways Satan Wins 4
How To Find A Church 5
The Three Sisters 6
Quarreling About Words 7
Prejudice In The Early Church 8
Of Myths And Fluff 9
Winning Teams 10
Two Wives 11

Personal

Our Daughter 14
Being Better Neighbors 16
Good Neighbors: Borrowing And Lending 17
Good Things About Alzheimer's 18

Creating Closer Families 20

The Old Ways 22

A Bum Or Not A Bum? 23

My Mother. 24

Mother's Day 26

Friends …Lost And Found. 27

Lost Friendship 28

Be Mentally Tough 29

The Churches I've Attended 30

Incredible Hospitality. 32

Parables

Two Farmers 36

Parable Of The Bad Farmer. 37

The Parable Of The Athletic Club 38

The Prodigal Daughter. 40

The Parable of the Wedding Banquet (Matthew 22) 41

When Is Jesus Coming? (Matthew 24–25) 42

Veterinary

The Parable of the Lost Dog 46

Something You Can Learn From Dogs 47

Lessons From Pets 48

CONTENTS

Healthy Immune Systems 50

Creation: Possibilities And Probabilities 52

Wayward Members 53

Jokes

No Joke 56

Flee Fornication 57

Talking Frogs 58

Managing Anger With Subjection 59

Parenting

Socialization 62

Respect or Anger? 64

How to Work 65

Scatter Shooting While Thinking About Parenting 66

Bible Study

Doctors, Preachers, and Other Specialists 70

Intellectual Dishonesty 71

Introductions and Conclusions 72

Interpreting Scripture: Understand Purpose 73

The Old Testament in Romans 74

CONTENTS

Prayer

Preparation for Prayer 76

The Days of Our Lives 77

Surprised By Prayer 78

Reasons Why God Doesn't Answer Prayer (James 4:3) 80

Spiritual Arrogance 81

Esther

A Few Thoughts About The Book Of Esther 84

The Book Of Esther 86

A Great Hero 87

Mordecai the Magnificent 88

Marriage

Marriage 101 92

45th Wedding Anniversary 94

Happiness and Sorrow 95

My Husband Doesn't Love Me 96

God Hates Divorce 97

Wild Cattle and Wild Husbands 98

A Glorious Wife 99

CONTENTS

Funerals

Emilio Sanchez Funeral 102

Glenn Torno Funeral 104

Ofeilia Guzman Funeral 106

Linda Magana Funeral 108

Evangelism

A Few Thoughts On Sharing God's Word With Other People . 110

Incredible Acts Of Heroism 111

"It's Easier To Believe The Bad Things" 112

Becoming Jesus 113

Helping The Lost 114

Edification for the Purpose of Evangelism 115

Arm Wrestling And Benevolence 116

Leadership

Nehemiah: Prayer, Planning and Preparation 118

More Leadership From Nehemiah (Nehemiah 2:12–13) 119

Wow, How, and Wow/How 120

Personal Growth

The Rich Man and Lazarus (Luke 16:19–31) 124

Criticism And Critics 125

Anniversary Parties...126

Spiritual Triage..127

Humility Contests...128

What To Do About Anger..129

Human Behaviors in Luke 9.....................................130

Satan And Peter...131

Why 40 Days In the Wilderness?................................132

Slaves And Slave Owners.......................................134

Stormy Seas And Faith...135

Thirty Pieces Of Silver.......................................136

What Must I Do To Inherit Eternal Life?.......................137

Making Grapes...138

Hospitality

Friendliness vs. Hospitality..................................140

Customer Service..141

Visitors ...Make The Most Of An Opportunity...................142

Perfect Hospitality...144

Three Cases of Hospitality....................................145

Elders

Eldership And Member Development..............................148

How To Discover And Develop Talent............................150

CONTENTS

Drought 151

Eldership and Wives. 152

Elder's Qualities 154

Eldership and Communicating Your Mission. 155

Eldership: Seating, Texting, etc. 156

Eldership And How the Church Functions 158

The Work Of Elders. 159

Elder Qualifications Retrospectively 160

My Advice To Young Men Concerning Preparing
 Themselves To Be Elders. 162

Bad And Good Shepherds. 163

Church

Building Us

Jesus, in John 17 while he was deep in prayer to his Father, prayed that his followers (you and I) would all be "one."

He wants us to bury pride and ego and live lives of service to each other...true humility. 1 Corinthians 12:26 adds further instruction to that concept. When one of the members is sad...all are sad. When one is happy...all are happy. We all understand these concepts but how should they be applied?

In 1998, when my father died, fourteen from Parkway made the three hour drive to attend his funeral. I was impressed with that then and I'm still impressed.

I understand the sacrifice that is made for such an effort and I'll never forget it. I also understand that I'm a pretty high profile member at Parkway. Let me urge this...when one of our members, perhaps of a lesser profile, loses a loved one...attend that funeral. If there is a sacrifice in time that needs to be made then to the best of your ability make that sacrifice. At funerals, all the façade of self-control is stripped away and you see people in their purest form with all their raw emotions exposed.

It is an experience that is huge in developing compassion and love for each other. Through those and other experiences we become a congregation that is a true family not just an assembly of casual acquaintances. Sometimes people will say, "Well I didn't know the deceased." No, but you do know your fellow Christian.

Parkway is a great congregation but we can make it better. It becomes better when every member decides to live a life of service, expressed in deeds, to every other member in the congregation.

Conflict In A Local Church And The Importance Of Leadership

Certainly we're all familiar with sinful conflict in a local church and how the scriptures instruct us to deal with that, but how about non-sinful conduct in a local church and how that is handled?

I'm talking about things like children running and playing and endangering the older folks. How about babies screaming in the assembly so that you can't listen to a prayer? Or a message board with a questionable message? How about kids who break a window with a ball?

What about visitors who wear shorts to services on Wednesday nights? How about cell phones that go off during the assembly? What about those who are chronically late to services? What about the teacher who leaves town without finding a substitute teacher to take their place? What about the songleader who leads songs that the congregation cannot sing, either because the congregation does not know the song or it is led in such a way that it is difficult to sing along with? What about the person who trims his nails during the assembly?

In the Veterinary business we deal with a parasite called a "hookworm." Left untreated, hookworms can cause death. We sometimes get the question, "How can I eliminate hookworms from my yard?" The answer is, "Spread rock salt over your yard." The trouble is that even though you destroy all the hookworms, you destroy everything else in the process and end up with a dead yard.

Here's the deal…conflict in a church is good and is to be expected. It means that people are interacting with each other and annoying each other. Members need to learn how to deal with each other. Sometimes elders interfere in that process and become so repressive that the congregation becomes like the yard treated with rock salt…a dead place.

There are ways to deal with hookworms and there are ways to deal with conflicts in a local church so that the culture of the church is preserved. Effective leadership finds a way.

Two Ways Satan Wins

In 1 Corinthians 5, the text reveals that one of the members of the Lord's church is in a sexual relationship with his father's wife. He is following his master...Satan. Paul condemns the members in that church for tolerating that sin and urged them to punish this member by casting him out of their Christian community...they were to have nothing to do with him. Satan was winning because he had won the individual who was committing the sin and he had damaged the church because outsiders looking in would ridicule God. Satan wins in this case because of their under-reaction to sin.

I don't know why the congregation tolerated this overt sinful behavior. Perhaps they thought that listening to a preacher every Sunday morning might eventually cause him to correct his behavior...I don't know but it was the wrong approach.

Of course the punishment had a design to it...it was designed to create remorse in the individual so he would realize what he had lost and quit having sex with his father's wife.

The second way Satan wins is by over-reaction to sin. Second Corinthians 2:7–11, has Paul warning the congregation not to over-do the punishment or the now sorrowful member might be overwhelmed by his sorrow and Satan wins again. The individual is so sorrowful that he becomes spiritually crippled and ineffective in his Christianity. He no longer is guilty of an active sin but is perhaps guilty of an inactive sin.

When a sheep is lost from the flock let's go find it and when we find it let's not berate and chastise it but build it up with a spirit of compassion.

Don't let Satan win.

Church

How To Find A Church

First of all when looking for a church it helps to have a little Bible knowledge. After all there were several New Testament churches that God was not happy with. Not happy at all. So it makes sense to see what kind of church God did not like.

You should want to be a member of a church that will help you grow as a Christian. That kind of church will hold you accountable for when you are falling a little short and encourage you to do better. When you do good they'll slap you on the back and be so proud of you and it will make you feel so good you'll want to do even better.

You should also want to be a member of a church that doesn't tolerate open and willful sin. I see plenty of churches where men and women are living together outside of vows of marriage. That's just not right. God doesn't like it and neither should we and you shouldn't want to be part of a church that tolerates anything like it.

When you look at a church look at it's people. A church ought to have people in it that have some long marriages. People who are true to their vows. Sometimes divorce can't be helped but a church should have some marriages in it that have weathered some storms. A church should be full of friendly welcoming people. Hospitality is big with the Lord…real big. If a church doesn't care about you when you visit, chances are she won't ever care much about you after you are a member there. A church ought to be full of people who have great Bible knowledge. After all it is just one book isn't it? God's people should love God's book and know it inside and out.

In short look for a church that is producing people who look like Jesus Christ. If it's not then, well…it's not much of a church.

The Three Sisters

I found out recently that my ancestry includes Native Americans. My people were accomplished farmers and believed in planting three inseparable plants together; corn, green beans and squash...called "The Three Sisters." They planted beans with corn because beans are nitrogen fixers. Beans take nitrogen from the atmosphere and add it to the soil thus fertilizing the corn plant. The squash have big broad leaves which serve to shade the soil and inhibit the growth of life sapping weeds. At the time of harvest my people would have good crops of corn, beans and squash.

This is similar to the needs of a new Christian. He needs the association with plants that can help him grow and make him better. Some Christians can help new Christians by helping them learn about God and give advice and encouragement. Other Christians can serve new Christians by providing them with new beneficial associations that replace the old sinful friends who have a tendency to pull new Christians back into their old destructive life styles. In addition, something wonderful and mysterious happens...the older, more mature Christian becomes energized and stronger...synergism.

Christians are mutually responsible to each other so God's crop of people can grow and be plentiful and be fruitful. What a wonderful plan God has...don't neglect it.

Quarreling About Words

Paul's letters to Timothy are carefully crafted to craft Timothy into an effective preacher/evangelist.

One of the problems Paul knew Timothy would face were members who would "quarrel about words." Keep in mind in those days there were no Bible dictionaries, concordances, wikipedia or any other kind of Bible reference resources. They just had the Old Covenant and letters written in their common language.

The same problem exists today. I've been in Bible classes that have taken three years to get through the letter to the Romans…blow by blow, verse by verse, examining every word ad nauseam…and perhaps missing the bigger message.

Sometimes members do argue and quarrel about words and relatively minor concepts. In my opinion, Bible classes are no place for arguing and quarreling which can create enmity. If you have a point make it and move on. If it needs any further discussion do it after class. Even after class don't go too far with it. If your brother doesn't agree with it, arguing is not going to solve the problem. Sometimes ideas just need time to permeate our brains.

Paul also instructs Timothy to "have nothing to do with foolish and stupid arguments." Yes, stupidity exists in churches. It's not hard to identify stupid people…minimize your contact with them…you probably can't make them smart.

In short, the Bible and God's message is not that hard to understand. The people in the first centuries could understand it and they didn't come close to having the Bible resources we have today.

Remember love God with all your heart, soul and mind and your neighbor as yourself. Part of loving God is to discover everything you can know about him. There are no shortcuts…study your Bible and personalize Paul's instructions to Timothy like he was writing to you.

Prejudice In The Early Church

During the early days of the church the Apostles had set up a "daily ministration" that included "serving tables" for widows. This probably would have been a central location where widows could come and be fed by members of the church. During the course of this problem arose between two classes of widows; "Hebrew" widows and "Grecian Jew" widows. These were Christian widows of course but the "Hebrew widows" would have been converts from Jews who had been raised in Judea and the "Grecian Jew widows" were those who had lived outside of Judea. In general, those Jews from Judea thought they were better than the Jews who were from other countries. They were prejudiced.

The problem was that some thought the Grecian Jew widows were being discriminated against at meal time. How might that happen? Well it might have been true. Maybe the Hebrew widows were getting the best tables or getting a bigger serving portion. Maybe they were getting seconds and the Grecian Jew widows weren't. Maybe those serving were more amiable toward the Hebrew widows than the Grecian Jew widows. Or maybe it wasn't true at all. Maybe the Grecian Jew widows were just very sensitive.

Wherever the problem lay...it was a problem and needed to be addressed and the apostles offered a solution that everyone agreed with. Sometimes in the church today we have similar problems. Let's do our best to not even give the appearance of discrimination but if there's a problem that we can't reconcile let's discuss it with the leaders of the congregation and hopefully we can find a solution that everyone can agree with.

Of Myths And Fluff

The apostle Paul instructed the young evangelist Timothy to…preach the word and in that preaching to correct, rebuke and encourage with great patience and instruction.

He warned Timothy that people will have a tendency to only want to listen to preachers that they like and that people have a tendency to listen to "myths" rather than the word of God.

I hear a lot of myths like…"God wants me to be happy and I'm not happy with this woman I'm married to so God wants me to find another woman." Or this myth…"Thinking about God sitting on a mountain top is better than attending a man-made church."

Those are webs that Satan (the great spider) has spun to catch people who won't tolerate sound gospel preaching.

Several years ago my son was looking at some old pictures of me and said…"Dad you're losing muscle mass." Those truthful words inspired me to go to the gym on a regular basis and start lifting weights.

However…the words I would have really liked to hear from my son (or anybody) is "Dad you look great"…but that would have been so much fluff. In retrospect I'm glad he was truthful with me.

There's a lot of fluff in the world…look for people who will tell you the truth about yourself. Find a church that doesn't just offer up spiritual cookies and cake. Find a church with a preacher like Timothy that will offer up a balanced spiritual diet and who will tell you the truth about yourself…so you can be the soldier God wants you to be.

UNCLE ROB'S BLOG

Winning Teams

There are a lot of similarities between the game of football and the church and her work.

- both are team oriented
- both rely not only on the abilities of their members but also how those abilities function within a group
- both have a goal or mission
- both can be evaluated on their performance
- both have people in a leadership position to keep their members focused, on task and motivated.

Coach Mike Sherman while coach of the Texas A&M football team noted that championship teams are built first in the locker room. That if you don't have a good locker room then regardless of the players individual abilities you won't have a winning football team. Football teams comprised of players with lesser abilities can out-perform teams comprised of players with greater abilities.

Congregations of Jesus Christ are like that as well. If the theory of Christianity is not reflected in our lives and how we interact with each other then we're not going to be very successful. If a church's members are angry with each other or jealous of each other or anything else that is inappropriate and sinful then it will not present well to the world and people can read that when they visit a congregation.

There are a lot of things that influence how a congregation performs but first and foremost congregations need to get there act together as it relates to controlling sin in our lives and appreciating and serving each other.

Church

Two Wives

In the Old Testament the nation of Israel was figuratively called God's wife. God was committed to his "wife" and cared for her and provided for her and she became prominent among the nations of the world. But there came a time when his wife wouldn't listen to him and she started following after "false" Gods. She committed adultery. God was patient and urged her to return to faithfulness to him but she rejected him. So God empowered a foreign nation to almost completely destroy her as punishment for her infidelity.

In the New Testament we see that Jesus Christ has a wife and his wife is the church. He cares for her and cherishes her and provides amply for her. However we read in the Book of Revelation (Chapters 1–3) that Jesus found fault with his wife. Among other things she had "left her first love," "followed after false teachings," and had become complacent in performing good works. Jesus warned her to make correction and if they did not he personally would "make war with them with the sword…"

God's bride Israel (of past times) and Christ's bride the church are beautiful brides as long as they remain faithful to their husband. It can be a beautiful and satisfying relationship. Jesus Christ will always be faithful as a husband to the church. As a church let's remember to be faithful to him in our good works and correct teaching of his Word.

Personal

Our Daughter

I attended my daughter's wedding today. Her mother and I thought she would never get married. Our friends have made the comment before that she would have a hard time finding a boy-friend because she is intimidating. In high school one of her teachers made the comment that they had never known a young lady as self-assured as Lauren. Add to that her intelligence (she graduated #23 in her class) and keen wit and charm and you might could understand why a young man would be intimidated.

Lauren used to say she didn't want to get married because she didn't want anyone telling her what to do. She and her best girlfriend agreed that they didn't want to change who they were just to catch a man.

Her mother and I are quite humorous in our own right but she has surpassed us both. Most people like to just sit around and listen to her.

She has been successful in her career. After graduation from Texas A&M University she came home and a temp agent placed her in an apartment leasing job for a major corporation. She was #2 in the nation in leasing that year. When she applied for a higher job within that same corporation and was turned down she asked me what to do. I told her to quit that job and find another one. She did but they wanted to keep her and gave her a job at the corporate head-quarters in which she excelled.

She is a young lady of the highest moral caliber. For her birthday one year she asked for all the Bible lesson books that Robert Harkrider had written and then jokingly wondered if they came with a Robert Harkrider action figure.

And then one day not quite a year ago she attended a Halloween party in the Austin area and a young man saw her and saw that wherever she went she was the center of attention and everyone was laughing and having fun around her. And that young man knowing only her name and where she worked tracked her down and sent her an email. The rest is history.

One of the preachers where they attend joked with Clark about the challenges of getting married to Lauren because of her strong mindedness. The young man told my daughter that was exactly why he loved her.

Today at the wedding I walked her down the aisle and gave her to that young man and I cried…unashamedly I cried.

Lauren wanted to make sure one thing was read at the wedding…

Ruth 1:15–17

> Then she said, "Behold, your sister-in-law has gone back to her people and her gods; return after your sister-in-law." But Ruth said, "Do not urge me to leave you or turn back from following you; for where you go, I will go, and where you lodge, I will lodge. Your people shall be my people, and your God, my God. Where you die, I will die, and there I will be buried. Thus may the Lord do to me, and worse, if anything but death parts you and me."

She never planned to change anything about herself but her mother and I can see that this young man's love is already changing her. We rejoice in who she is and who she will be. Thank you God.

UNCLE ROB'S BLOG

Being Better Neighbors

You know in David's class last night he asked the question, "Why aren't we saving more lost souls?" The answer was found in 1 Corinthians 9...service...

At the end of class I made the comment that another reason is that we aren't that different than non-Christians.

Here is an example. My neighbor, Sam Celum, mows 2 acres just like I do. I noticed the other day he was using his push mower. I talked to him and found out that his riding mower was broken and he was going to try to replace the engine on it. I told him he could use my riding mower any time he wanted. He said..."no he would just keep using the push mower."

I walked away feeling like I had done my duty as a neighbor and as a Christian.

Tonight about 7 pm I was out with my chain saw trimming up my oak trees when I noticed Sam pushing that mower through grass that was about 12 inches tall. I thought, "Sam really needs to buy a riding mower" and continued trimming my trees. Then I saw Sam's other neighbor, Mike come over with his riding mower and start helping Sam. I thought, "Doh...I wish that was me!" and I felt ashamed because Mike was a better neighbor than me.

Julie came out and I related to her my feelings and she told me to get my mower and help...it wasn't too late...so I did. See, Mike's not even a Christian. I never see him going to church. Usually he's sitting on his front porch with a can of beer in his hand. Often times in areas of service we're not any better than non-Christians.

We're going to have to really work hard to be different than the rest of the world. Here's another lesson. You can offer to help someone but oftentimes it's better just to help without asking. See a need and fulfill it. The benefit of helping others is not primarily for them...it's for you and me...it turns us into better people and we might convert a lost soul along the way.

Good Neighbors: Borrowing And Lending

I've reached the age where I don't really like to borrow things from people. Oh, I'm a good lender…and if you borrow from me I'll make you feel like I'm your best friend…but me borrowing…that's a different story.

Today I was riding my lawnmower and noticed that it was gouging my yard. I didn't really want to go buy another lawn mower so I called my friend Juan. Juan repairs small engines and he and I have developed a friendship. He's one of the few people I will borrow from. So I called Juan and told him about my problem and asked him if he had a riding lawnmower I could rent. Juan replied, "I've got one you can use." That's Juan-talk for he won't take any money.

I mowed my two acres with Juan's riding mower and when I was finished I blew all the dust off of it, sprayed it down with a pressure washer and filled the gas tank up all the way. I'm returning that mower better than I received it. That's being a good neighbor. Be a good neighbor when you borrow something. Don't return borrowed equipment back with only one drop of gasoline left in it and so caked with dirt you can't recognize it.

I know Juan won't take money from me but I'll tell him something like…"take your wife out to eat on me" or if that doesn't work I'll give him some flea products for his dogs (he's got 14 of them). Good friends take care of each other.

UNCLE ROB'S BLOG

Good Things About Alzheimer's

Alzheimer's is a horrible and dreadful disease. Julie's dad has it and it has stripped him of his memory and left him a shell of his former self. He has a hard time recognizing those who he has loved the most in the world and after a lifetime of being the "rock" in the family...he cannot care for himself and is wholly dependent on others to survive. The pathetic thing about Alzheimer's is that it doesn't kill you very quickly. Your body can continue surviving long after your brain is gone.

Another pathetic thing about Alzheimer's is that some families will not sign "do not resuscitate" orders so that some of these totally incapacitated folks are surviving, in name only, with stomach tubes and IV catheters in place. Trying to keep a body alive that wanted to die a long time ago.

So what's good about Alzheimer's? Seeing the love and compassion that is displayed by family members caring for their loved ones. That is a wonderful thing.

When Julie's dad was first diagnosed with Alzheimer's she drove to Houston every week to help her mother care for her dad. That went on for several months. Now that he is somewhat stabilized and the family has adjusted to his situation she is able to go once a month.

Last Sunday we went to go visit her dad and I was able to observe a part of her life that I had not known previously. She has come to know on a first name basis many of the patients there...and she helps and cares for them.

When we went down the hall to see her dad a woman in a wheel chair was screaming for help. Julie called her by name and asked her what was the matter and helped her...even though it interrupted the time she was spending with her dad. Countless times she pointed out people to me and told me their names and what was the matter with them. She also told me some of the people were missing...obviously passed from their earthly existence since the last time she was there.

Those folks are very aware of when dinner time is and if they are able, they start slowly moving in the direction of the dining hall. Julie was pushing her dad in his wheel chair and an old incapacitated man was wedged with his wheel chair in a corner. Julie said, "Rob, you push Daddy... I'll help him." When we got in the dining hall there were about 10 people already there and she started helping them put their bibs on. Those who were able smiled and thanked her.

Julie pointed out to me a cupholder that her brother Lonnie had attached to her dad's wheelchair. As I looked around I saw that there were other wheel chairs with those same cupholders attached.

Alzheimer's is a terrible disease and deservedly so, but the good thing about it is that it provides an opportunity for God's people to shine and when God's people are shining... God is glorified and... that's good.

UNCLE ROB'S BLOG

Creating Closer Families

A few years ago I created four private family Facebook pages: the family of Weldon and Nell Perkins, the Family of Charles and Naomi Norris, the Family of Clarke and Nellie Bedwell and the Family of Julian and Thelma Jackson.

I started with the Perkins family group because I wanted a format where we could share family stories and such like that we couldn't share with anyone else because they might view us as Martians or something worse. The world is really not ready to hear the shenanigans that go on in our family. My other motivation was to have a format whereby we could reconnect with each other and draw our family closer to each other (scattered as we are).

I then created the other family groups to help those families. The Norris family is my mother's family. The Bedwells and Jacksons are Julie's family.

I do most of the posting on those pages, sharing old family photos and letters and things going on in our lives. Other members of the families have gradually started posting.

The end result is our families are closer. Family members have become "friends" on Facebook who have never met each other. When we had the big Perkins family reunion in San Diego this summer, I heard several people say to each other…"you know I have never met you but I feel like I know you because of our friendship on Facebook."

This year we have gotten Christmas cards from family members that we have never gotten before. The in-laws of the Perkins family say things like "I have always wanted to be part of a big happy family."

Julie's annual family reunion in Kansas has benefitted. Many of them have told me…"Thank you for helping to make our family closer." Being the rascal that I am they take great pleasure in making fun of me. That common activity also makes them closer.

When we got together at my brother Greg's house for thanksgiving the three patriarchs (me, Scott and Greg) each gave a message to our family. Mine was that the Perkins family was special, that although we might occasionally have "issues" with each other that we still loved each other and didn't allow it to harm the family.

Everyone wants a closer happier family...build a private page and communicate a good message to each other. You might be surprised about how good it can get.

The Old Ways

I own a White Mountain hand crank ice cream machine. Most people use electric ice cream machines…not me…mine has to be cranked by hand. It takes 20 – 30 minutes to make ice cream. Julie keeps threatening to buy an electric one but I won't let her. I prefer to crank mine by hand. Years ago I heard from an old guy that when tractors first came out that many farmers were resistant to them. They said things like, "I can make a better crop with mules than with tractors" or "If you buy a tractor then you have to go and buy gas."

Some people like the old ways and are resistant to change. I'm that way about church too…I believe in the old ways…the Bible ways; singing without instrumental accompaniment, baptism by immersion, taking the Lord's Supper every week, etc.

Cranking ice cream by hand or farming with mules is a personal choice that we can do or not do, but things related to church come from God. God knows what kind of worship he wants and we should respect that.

I like to hand crank ice cream because it reminds me of good times at my grandparents house when I would take turns with my cousins turning that crank. Those memories are pleasing and precious to me. I worship God the old way because it pleases Him and pleasing Him pleases me too.

Personal

A Bum Or Not A Bum?

Walker and I were pulling my boat out of the water on Tuesday and a guy that looked like a bum walked up and tried to sell us a few things. He looked like a bum but he had an old car…most bums have no transportation. He needed to sell some things because he needed to buy gas. The trouble was I didn't really want anything he had so I just handed him a five dollar bill. His response surprised me he said he wasn't looking for a handout.

I said, "That's okay, you're not a bum. I just don't need anything you have and I want to help you." He walked away and came back with a pocket knife and gave it to me and said he couldn't just take my money.

Lesson learned…just because a guy looks like a bum doesn't mean he is. Thank you Lord…I needed that lesson.

My Mother

If you see me riding my riding lawn mower you might notice that I occasionally cry. I'm not sad about harming the grass but it is a time when I'm engaged in a mindless activity and can reflect on things. This morning I was reflecting on my mother…Naomi Geviene Norris Perkins. I guess growing up I didn't really fully appreciate how special she was. We kind of got to grow up together. She had me 4 days before her 17th birthday.

A lot of people were always attracted to mom. She was always the most beautiful mom but the best part of her was her engaging personality. She was always full of life and fun. She made friends at the drop of a hat. We lived all over the country (California, Utah, Alabama, Virginia and Texas) and she made life-long friends wherever we lived. Many people coming to Houston for treatment at MD Anderson stayed in the home of my parents. One summer two college students were selling dictionaries and they ended up living with us for a summer. We also had a foster child living with us for a while.

She was always interested in things. She grew and cultivated African violets; she designed and modeled dresses and she loved to cook.

She was our Bible class teacher, our den mother and was active in the PTA. She would whip us when we were bad and laugh with us and hug us. There was a lot of love in our family. She taught us early on how to cut up a chicken. And she was hospitable. It seemed like every Sunday after church she and dad were bringing someone home for lunch. And every Thanksgiving and Christmas we had company.

She loved my dad's family. She called Dad's parents "Ma and Pa." All the nephews and nieces, because they couldn't pronounce "Aunt Geviene" very well, called her "Aunt Weenie."

We never missed church…ever! In fact when mom was a new Christian and I was in the hospital to get my tonsils out…left the hospital so she could attend Wednesday night Bible study. Of course now she can't believe she did that.

A lot of people wished my mom was their mom. And for a lot of them she was.

Mom is incredibly compassionate and forgiving and always wants to believe the best in people. Some people have treated her awfully but she forgives and forgets.

She has buried two husbands who loved and adored her... Bob Perkins and Darrel Roberts.

And now as she has aged and weathered all these years and can no longer live in her home. A home full of memories and treasures must be said goodbye to. I've hauled a lot of things to my home that some would consider junk but each item, like the old pogo stick, has a special memory for me. To say it's traumatic would be an understatement. But the two most important things in Mom's life are family and church. She'll live just down the road from Greg and Kristi and many grandchildren and be able to go to church with them three times a week. And she'll have family to take her to the doctors and care for her.

I have an incredible mom and today is her birthday. A large part of who I am is because of her and I know it very well. Happy birthday to an incredible Mom.

Mother's Day

I don't know when my mom started getting old but one day I noticed her moving slower and being quieter and just kind of being content being in the back ground and that's not my mom. Since that time I find myself thinking about her all the time and dreading the day that I won't have her anymore. I guess that realization has caused some changes in me. I find myself calling her a lot more. I found out she talked on the phone to her sister every day so I decided what's important to mom is also important to me so now one of my routines is to call aunt Missie on a regular basis and visit with her. I've learned a lot about my mom from her sister.

Aunt Missie told me the other day that mom was the smartest of the three siblings. When I told mom that she said, "no aunt Missie is the smartest…" they love each other. I feel sorry for which ever one lives the longest. There is no joy in being the last one alive.

The other day Mom was down visiting and after supper she was in the kitchen helping clean up and my oldest grandchild (5 years old in a month) went in to the kitchen and told her "grandma, come play with us …we hardly ever get to see you." Then on the way home Victoria asked my son and his wife where my mom lived and could she maybe come to Corpus Christi and live with them. I can't tell you how much I love my granddaughter for making my mother feel so loved.

I am who I am today because my mother is who she is and I know that fact well. There will be a day when she's gone and I can't see her anymore or talk to her or share things with her but until that day comes I'm going to make the rest of her days as special as I can. Thanks Mom for everything.

Friends ... Lost And Found

I know two people who love each other and each wants to feel important to the other person...and yet they don't call each other because they think the other person should call them. So two people who could have a much deeper relationship...don't because of their expectations.

A long time ago when I was a deacon I was really close to one of our elders and then some church trouble came up and we found ourselves on different sides of the fence. The troubles were resolved but our relationship was never the same and then the old elder and his wife moved away. I loved that old man...he had taught me a lot about the Lord and plus we were just good friends.

I hated it that we had lost our old friendship and then one day I told Julie, "I don't care if he doesn't like me...I like him" and I started calling him and talking with him and lo and behold our friendship rekindled and I found out that he had never stopped liking me and it just took me a little effort to find that out.

Carl Miller developed Alzheimer's and no longer lives on this earth. I'm glad that we found our relationship before it was too late.

Put your pride away and call those people you love.

Lost Friendship

Several years ago at Parkway when I was a young deacon one of the elders took me under his wing and showed some interest in me. We would go visit members who needed to be visited and plus we were just good friends…we ate together, we fished and we played dominoes. And then one day some trouble visited the church and he and I ended up on opposite sides of it. We were never in direct conflict with each other but it changed our friendship.

Shortly after that he retired and moved off. I missed the comradeship I had with the old man but I guess what I missed more was just calling him on the phone and talking…I still miss that. I was afraid he didn't like me anymore and it bothered me…bothered me a lot. I asked a close friend what I should do and they said…"If he liked you he would call you."

But then I thought…that's a two way street and decided I don't care if he likes me or not…I still like him and I'm going to call. Boy howdy I'm glad that I did because it was just like old times. We would talk about the church and the people and I cherished that I had my old friend back.

The old man is dead now and has been dead for a while but I haven't forgotten him and I'm glad that I did something to make his last years a little easier.

If you're walking in the same shoes I was you might give some thought to doing a simple thing like picking up the phone and making a call it can be awfully good medicine for a broken relationship.

Personal

Be Mentally Tough

I first started playing volleyball about thirty years ago and found out I loved the sport. The only problem was I was the worst player on the court and the other players let me know it...not by overt words but things like body language and other expressions of contempt. Often times the better players will hit hard balls at inferior players to run them off.

I experienced all those things but...I loved volleyball and I told myself and reassured myself that all I needed was time and repetition to develop the needed skill set. To be successful at anything you have to develop mental toughness.

You have to be mentally tough to be a good Christian too. You may take a long look at your life and compare it to someone else's and decide you need Christ and Christianity. You may even love the Christian life but find that there are those who criticize you...maybe even people you love the most in the world. They may say things like...Christians are hypocrites or...that church is a cult. They may look at the things you're trying to correct and control in your life and tempt you with those same things.

I knew a young man who wanted to go to church on Sunday mornings but his wife would offer to be intimate with him if he stayed home...so he stayed home.

If you're going to be a Christian you have to be mentally tough and have faith in God's plan to turn you into who you need to be. You have to build new habits and you may have to lose a few old friends...but let me tell you this...whatever you have to give up will pale in comparison to what you will be blessed with.

I turned 65 last year and this month I'm going to a volleyball tournament in San Antonio to qualify for the U.S. Nationals in Florida. I gave myself time to develop the skills I needed, I ignored all the naysayers and I never gave up on the sport I love or myself.

Study your Bibles, grow in faith, congregate with your fellow Christians and get rid of all those friends who want you to fail and we'll march into heaven together.

The Churches I've Attended

I was born in San Diego, California in 1954. Mother and Dad attended Johnson Street Church of Christ. We moved away when I was in the first grade. Of course I was just a kid but I remember all my parents friends were Christians. They were always in the homes of their friends and we had a lot of company as well. They would always be some of the last people to leave because they would stay so long visiting.

Next we lived in Brigham City, Utah and attended a church of Christ. It was pretty small as most of the people who lived there were Mormons. We met in some kind of schoolhouse. We would get there early and set out chairs and put them up after services. The classes were in the basement that was accessed by a trap door. When we would get out of class we would climb the stairs and lift the door up with our heads while the adults were still having their class. I remember we went on something called an encampment with the other members and we camped and cooked outside. Dad said this church was a "liberal" church but was too poor to spend their money in a "liberal" way.

When I was in the fourth grade we moved to Athens, Alabama. It seemed like there were churches of Christ on every street corner and we went to a big one. We only lived there for a year (1965) and I don't remember much about it. I do remember that the members would stop by and visit occasionally and I attended Athens Bible School.

Then we moved to Annandale, Virginia to another small church that met in a schoolhouse. I threw a snowball and broke out a window at the school. I don't remember getting in trouble for it. Very friendly people there and I was baptized when I was in the 8th grade. Of course Mother and Dad were some of the most active members in whatever church we attended and in most of them they were always the youngest couple.

Round about 1968 we moved to Houston, Texas and attended at Spring Branch Church of Christ. It seemed huge…maybe about 300 members. The church had elders and deacons and was a fantastic church. I was 6'-1" in the eighth grade and we first attended on a Wednesday night. A lot of the girls were interested in me until they found out how young I was. Houston at the time was the longest we had lived anywhere. I had plenty of friends my age at church and we ran around together. Mother had company every Sunday for lunch. Dad became a deacon there and they let me lead songs on Sunday morning. Men like Roy Cogdill, Kent Ellis, Maurice Jackson, and Robert Harkrider preached while we were there.

I met Julie there one Sunday morning in Bible class and made many life-long friends. The church split after I went to college and there was a lot of heartache over that.

Julie and I married and moved to College Station, Texas to attend school. We attended Twin City Church of Christ for the eight years we were up there. We attended on a regular basis and I led songs, etc. David Smitherman and Joe Fitch preached while we were there and we became life-long friends.

After graduation (1981) our young family…Julie, Walker and I moved to Mexia, Texas where we attended Shiloh Church of Christ…another small church. We had some friends up there and that's part of the reason we moved there. Almost the minute we stepped in the door they asked me if I would teach the auditorium class. We were and still are close to the Lucas family who live there. Joe Lucas was my dad's best friend.

In 1982 we moved to Corpus Christi (Julie was pregnant with Lauren) where we remain to this date (2020). This congregation owns my heart and is my life's work. I became a deacon and elder here. When we moved here Elmer Moore was preaching followed by Charles Boshart, Sakkie Pretorius, David Smitherman and now Marc Hinds. I have served as an Elder with David, Gus Cargile, Bill Chambers and Ricardo Baca. We raised our kids in this congregation and now all six of our grandkids are here as well.

If you think I don't know I've been blessed…well…you're wrong about that. Sometimes it's good to look back at where you've been and the people and experiences that have shaped you and I thank God…and you for that.

Incredible Hospitality

Ken Osbourne visited recently and I was reminded of the hospitality Parkway showed to us when we came here. In 1982 I was working in a predominately beef cattle practice in Mexia, Texas and looking for a better paying job. I heard of one in Corpus Christi so I set up an interview. Julie's Dad knew a member of the Church in Corpus, John Osborne, and told us the Osborne's wanted us to stay with them. We don't usually stay with strangers but since we were dirt poor we agreed to. So we got in our 1974 Dodge Charger, that burned more oil than gas, and headed for Corpus. Julie was six months pregnant and Walker was about 3 years old. We reached Refugio, Texas about 11:00 at night and didn't want to be a burden to the Osborne's so we called and said we were getting in late and would just find a hotel. Brother Osborne told me all the hotels were full and they would wait up for us...he wouldn't take no for an answer. So we rolled in after midnight, met them and went right to bed.

The next morning I was at Riverside Veterinary Clinic interviewing all day, which meant watching Dr. Denman work his clinic until about noon. Then we grabbed a hamburger and I went with him on a farm call to see a sick cow. On the way back we came to an agreement and I drove to the Osborne's house. Keep in mind this was before cell phones and I hadn't talked to Julie all day long. When I got there I told Julie I had taken the job and she told me that the Osborne's were throwing us a party that night, that there were some people in the church that we had known from our A&M days. So that night they had a houseful; Brad & Beth Roach and Tim & Dorothy Torno were young couples we had known from A&M. And of course we made many life-long friends that night; Carl & Dot Miller, Elmer Moore, Hutchins, Barnes, Ray Tornos, Dansbys, Grafs, etc.

We went to church the next morning and afterwards Brother Osborne took me around looking at rent houses. We rented a place that Sunday where one of the malls stands now. The rental company would not take my out of town check so Carl Miller took our check and gave me cash and we were able to put a deposit on that rent house. Julie reminded me that

Personal

Linda Torno came to the rent house with her kids after we left and saw the condition of the back yard and cleaned up a lot of broken glass and other trash. Of course, we moved in July 4th week-end and Lauren was born Aug 31. Four weeks later the church ladies had a baby shower. Julie said she held Lauren and let Walker open the gifts and he kept expecting a truck or a motorcycle but kept getting something pink until finally one of those thoughtful church ladies handed him a present that contained something for him. God bless them. Incredible hospitality which we will never forget and I was reminded of when Ken Osborne visited last.

Parables

Two Farmers

There were two farmers who made a crop every year but they approached farming in two drastically different ways.

The first farmer was an old school farmer. He owned a farm that his father and grandfather had farmed before him. He liked the old ways of farming. He liked hooking the harnesses up to the mules and following them as they plowed. Sometimes his young sons would ride on his shoulders as he plowed. He saved seed back every year from the harvest. As the young plants would come up he and his family would hoe the rows to keep the weeds down and at harvest the whole family would be in the fields picking cotton. They worked from sun-up to sun-down and took pride in their work. He knew there were newer ways to farm but was satisfied to farm the way he was the most comfortable with.

The second farmer was also raised on a family farm but when tractors became available he made the switch. Eventually he was using tractors that were guided by GPS systems. He invested in hybrid seeds that produced plants that were both drought and herbicide resistant. When it came time to control weeds he was able to overspray his fields with herbicide that didn't harm the cotton plants. When harvest time came the big combines would come in collect all that cotton in a jiffy. Because his operations were so profitable he was able to expand his operations and farm more land and became even more productive.

The farmers are elders and preachers. The farms represent both the lost in the world and local congregations. Some of the elders and preachers like the old ways…tried and true and do some good. Some of them look at the changes that are occurring in society and are reaching out to society where society "gathers"…like social media and instead of going "door to door" are using the internet to teach classes on Skype. There are many tools to build congregations and find the lost. Let's seek them out and use them.

Parable Of The Bad Farmer

There was a farmer who inherited his dad's farm after his dad passed away. His dad loved farming and hard work and made a good crop every year. The son however didn't share his dad's love or passion for farming. Oh...he liked being called a farmer but instead of spending his time out in the fields he liked to dress up in his boots and hat and go down to the coffee shop and talk with some of the other farmers. He also liked big shiny tractors so he traded his dad's old tractor for a newer model with air conditioning and GPS. He didn't really care too much if his crops failed because he had crop insurance. In fact since crop insurance would return about 75% of the estimated value of the crop...instead of praying for rain he would pray that it didn't rain. He could live on the 75%. He wasn't the farmer his dad was.

The Lord's church needs leaders who love the church like Christ loved the church. The church needs leaders who are innovative and actively engaged and have a passion for servant leadership. You can grow a good crop with the right kind of leadership.

The Parable Of The Athletic Club

There were three men who were plagued with being over-weight and its attended side effects; type II diabetes, cardiovascular problems and just not being able to live the kind of lives physically that they wanted to.

They all three joined a gym. The first one started controlling his diet and seven days a week was on the elliptical machine. By the end of the year he had lost all his weight, his diabetes went away and his cardiovascular symptoms were greatly improved. He had a problem though…he had not done anything to improve the quality of his muscles and looked like a walking stick. He was still physically weak.

The second guy changed his diet and was drinking and eating a lot of protein and limiting his carbs and fats. He spent all his time lifting weight and building muscle mass. At the end of the year he had transformed himself…his diabetes went away and his cardiovascular symptoms were improved. His problem though was he was almost grotesque in the muscle mass he had accumulated and with the smallest amount of exertion got "winded." He had neglected doing "cardio."

The third guy listened to his trainer and on even days lifted weights and on odd days did his cardio. At the end of the year he was the perfect combination of form and function. His diabetes and cardiovascular symptoms went away and physically he could do what he wanted.

The parable is this. All three guys had lived their lives without God. Their spiritual health was near zero. They determined to change that and went looking for God and visited three different churches.

The first church emphasized Bible study but gave no encouragement or example in interacting with sinners and performing works of service. Its members by and large were giants in Bible knowledge but midgets in works of service, i.e. the skinny guy.

The second church emphasized works and were socially active but had minimal Bible study and doctrinally accepted anything. They were by and large giants in works of service but midgets in the knowledge of God, i.e. the muscle bound guy.

The third church took a balanced approach. They emphasized Bible study but also encouraged, by word and by example, works of service. It had an incredibly symbiotic effect. Works of service helped in the understanding of God's word and created an individual that mimicked Jesus Christ himself...perfect in form and in function.

Who do you want to be?

UNCLE ROB'S BLOG

The Prodigal Daughter

Remember in Luke 15:11–32, the very emotional story of the "Prodigal Son?" The son claimed his inheritance from his father and with that money he went to another country and wasted it in "riotous living." Finally he was broke and starving. No one would help him. He decided he would go back home and tell his dad he was sorry and ask to be a servant on the farm. When his dad saw him far off down the road, he recognized his lost son and ran to him and hugged and kissed him. The boy said to him, "Father I have sinned against heaven, and in thy sight: I am no more worthy to be called son." The father turned to his servants and said, go get the best clothes, put a ring on his finger and shoes on his feet: bring the fatted calf…we're going to have a party…"for this my son was dead, and is alive again; he was lost, and is found."

This is a very emotional story about forgiveness and how we treat those who want forgiveness. I love that story.

Let's change it up a little. Let's make the Prodigal Son a Prodigal Daughter.

She wastes her life in "riotous living." She recognizes her sin and decides to go back to her Dad. He sees her and runs up to her and hugs her neck and kisses her. She asks for forgiveness and then looks down and notices she is…pregnant. What happens next?

My guess is the old man is so happy to have his "dead" daughter back that he does just for her what he would do for the son…even if she is pregnant.

I tell this story because sometimes when a girl gets pregnant out of wedlock we think we have to treat her differently. Somehow she has to know that she has sinned, and throwing a party or a baby shower might mute that message or perhaps encourage other girls to get pregnant out of wedlock. I think we think too much sometimes. The joy of recovering a loved one lost in sin should be so joyous that we want to send the message…you are completely forgiven…welcome back daughter. That's consistent with Luke 15.

The Parable of the Wedding Banquet (Matthew 22)

In this parable Jesus weaves a story about a King who is throwing a wedding party for his son. He had his "A" list of invitees but they refused to come. So he sent the invitation again, this time with more details…fattened beef cooked to perfection, etc. They still refused to come and went about their own business.

Some of them seized the King's messengers and mistreated and killed some of them. The King was so mad he sent his army and killed those murderers and destroyed their city.

Then he told his messengers to go out among his kingdom and find whoever they could to come to the party. It didn't matter who they were. At last the wedding hall was filled to capacity.

As the King was intermingling with the guests he came across a fellow that wasn't dressed appropriately. The King told his servants to tie him up and throw him into outer darkness…for many are called but few are chosen.

The King is God. The wedding party is the uniting of Jesus Christ (his son) with his bride the church (God's people).

The first guests invited were the Jews. They rejected God's invitation and killed his messengers (John the Baptist, etc.).

God destroyed them and their city (Jerusalem) in AD 70.

The next guests who were invited were the sinners and the Gentiles (the rest of humanity). Unlike the Jewish establishment they were glad to come to the party. However, some of them didn't abide by God's rules…they didn't give up sin and were unsuitable to be at the party.

You see this wasn't just a wedding party they were invited to…they were invited to marry Jesus Christ the Son of God…to become "one flesh" with him. But they didn't recognize him and they didn't understand the unspeakable value of the gift they were turning down.

God still invites humanity to be in a spiritual relationship with his Son…don't pass it up or you will be really, really sorry.

UNCLE ROB'S BLOG

When Is Jesus Coming? (Matthew 24–25)

This section begins with Jesus prophesying about the destruction of Jerusalem in A.D. 70 with undertones of the day of judgement. Then we read of two parables before we get to a section that is definitely talking about the final judgement day.

In the final Judgement Day Jesus specifically details the requirements for entering the eternal kingdom. Namely...feeding the hungry, giving drink to the thirsty, taking in strangers, clothing those who need clothes, visiting the sick and visiting those in prison.

So now let's look at the parables.

The first one is the parable of the 10 virgins. They had a job...one job...to carry oil fueled torches to lead the bridegroom into the wedding feast. The problem was that the bridegroom didn't come when they expected. Five of the virgins were prepared for that eventuality...they brought extra oil. They got to go into the marriage feast. The others didn't.

The bridegroom is Jesus, the virgins are Christians and the wedding feast is heaven. You have to be prepared when Jesus comes. You have to have enough oil when Jesus comes. The oil is helping the hungry, thirsty, strangers, unclothed, sick and prisoners. You can't stop engaging in those activities and rest on your laurels or like with the 5 foolish the door to the wedding feast will be slammed in your face.

The second parable is about the 5, 2 and 1 talent men. Their master trusted them with money based on their ability and then came back for an accounting. The 5 and 2 talent doubled their money and are invited to "enter into the joy" of their Lord. The one talent man is too lazy to work for the master and returns his investment to him. The master cast the 1 talent man into "outer darkness."

Jesus is the master; the servants are Christians. Entering into the master's joy is heaven and being condemned to "outer darkness" is hell. The investment the master makes in them is the investment Jesus makes in us.

The investment is helping the hungry, thirsty, strangers, unclothed, sick and prisoners.

To sum it up Christians need to be continually doing good because they don't know exactly when Jesus is coming. In addition, God has an investment in us that is guaranteed to produce if we will just try. That's all he asks is effort.

Heaven and hell are waiting. Choose where you want to go by your actions. Don't be lazy.

Veterinary

The Parable of the Lost Dog

An older widow woman had lost her dog. She had had that dog since it was a puppy. It had been with her when her husband got sick and after he died. When she got home from the funeral she sat on the couch and cried her eyes out. That little dog snuggled up to her and was a great comfort during her sorrow...and now it was gone. So she started walking the streets looking for it. She knocked on all her neighbor's doors looking for it and couldn't find it. She didn't get much sleep that night.

The next morning she put out posters with a reward for anyone who would find her little dog. She went to the dog pound. She went to all the veterinary offices...and she prayed. A few days later she had a knock on her door and there were three kids with a little dog in their arms. The little dog jumped into her arms and licked her in the face. The woman wept for joy. She grabbed that little dog and just held it and never wanted to let go of it.

That's how we ought to act when a person is sorry for their sins. It shouldn't matter what the sin was or who it might have hurt or how many times they might have failed before. We should rejoice and maybe cry and maybe just want to hold them because that's how God feels about us when we come back to him.

Look for the lost with all your effort, don't give up and when you find them don't be ashamed to rejoice.

Something You Can Learn From Dogs

I was recently at a seminar that provides service dogs for people who are handicapped and often wheelchair bound. I was struck by what the speaker said, that a lot of these handicapped people are mentally beat down because they are not normal and that feeling is validated every day by the way people look at them and treat them. When this organization provides a service dog for these individuals a transformation begins to take place…the dog provides unconditional love…the dog cannot see the handicap. He's blind to it.

And eventually the handicapped person begins to believe the dog that they are worthy of love.

Jesus Christ provides that kind of transforming love but the problem with that is it's hard to buy into concepts. What's easier to buy into is when the Lord's people provide that kind of unconditional love. Then it becomes palpable and real and helps build faith in Jesus Christ.

So when we meet someone who is not like us and may wear the visible effects of a sin stained life don't look at that handicap, don't even look at it…look at the person inside and use the power of love that Jesus gave you to help transform them because eventually they'll begin to believe in it and reject the lie that Satan has sold them and believe in Jesus Christ.

UNCLE ROB'S BLOG

Lessons From Pets

Sometimes when I examine a dog at work the client says something like this, "I'm spending more money on my dog than I do on my kids!" I usually respond by saying, "Yeah but this dog will never talk back to you or break your heart."

I have watched Julie over the years with our pets. Our dogs and cats love her. They want to be in whatever room she is in. They want to sit on the couch by her. She talks to them and they listen. She can read their expressions and know what they want. It's always very emotional for both of us when their health deteriorates so much that we have to put one of them to "sleep." When our Sheltie "Suzy" had to be put to sleep for lung cancer, Julie asked me to bring the shot home because Suzy gets nervous up at the clinic. Julie held Suzy in her arms at home while I administered the euthanasia solution, she died very peacefully. We both cried.

What makes people love their pets so much? And is there anything we husbands can learn from that?

People love their pets because no matter how horrible of a mood we might be in…they are still happy to see us. Sometimes I go into an exam room where there is a lab puppy who is jumping up and down and wanting to lick me and just sooo happy…I tell the client…"this is how my wife acts when I get home from work every day." Imagine if that were true .

People love their pets because their pets want to be with them. You husbands think about this…your wife needs you to be with her. It might mean you have to sacrifice some of your precious time…just to be with her. Maybe just watching some dumb movie with her. No one needs that lesson more than I do.

People love their pets because their pets think they are the greatest people in the world. It's easy to tell your wife that you love her, but those are empty words if she can't see it in your actions. Convince her with your actions that no one on earth is more important than she is.

Veterinary

I wish every one of you could have a loving pet and experience them from puppyhood to old age and failing health. They can teach you a lot about the shortness of life and how to care for each other.

UNCLE ROB'S BLOG

Healthy Immune Systems

We see a lot of Parvo virus in young dogs, frequently, every single day. Distraught owners will come in with pathetic little puppies ravaged by vomiting and diarrhea. I explain to our clients that I don't have any medications that will kill the virus that our treatment is a supportive treatment to build the puppy up so its own immune system can fight off the virus. Hospitalized puppies who survive can be sick for seven days. Even with those meds and bills that can be over $1000; we can't save them all.

Puppies are very susceptible because they have weak and developing immune systems. I've had families crying their eyes out over their sick pets. The sad thing about this illness is it can easily be prevented through relatively inexpensive vaccination.

I'm a keen observer of why people visit churches they've never darkened the door to. I've seen people come in who have a sick child with a poor prognosis. All of a sudden it's time to find God and invoke his healing power.

I have also seen folks whose lives are a mess…marital problems, parental problems, etc. Again it's time to find Jesus.

Many times when the problem goes away or calms down, so do peoples' spiritual interest. They quickly revert back to the way they were living until the "problem" resurfaces again.

Folks, who are responsible purchase a new puppy, control their internal and external parasites, put them on a good plane of nutrition and don't let that developing puppy hang out with other dogs until they are fully vaccinated. Those puppies rarely get sick.

Folks, who want to have good lives look for God early and develop a relationship with him and with his people. They go to Bible classes and feed themselves spiritually, they limit their associations with people who might be bad influentially, they live according to biblical principles and generally they don't get spiritually sick. Oh, Christians are going to suffer the same physical illnesses that everyone else does and there are going to be family problems, too. But they have vaccinated themselves against Satan and their spiritual immune systems are strong enough to survive the fiercest attack. They have built a relationship with God who is carefully listening and eagerly waiting to answer the prayers of his true children.

Don't be like that young puppy that may have only a 60% chance of survival. Be like that fully vaccinated and well cared for puppy that can live life to the fullest and bring many years of joy to its family.

Seek God early and often…he won't fail you.

Creation: Possibilities And Probabilities

When I was in veterinary school they taught us that as diagnosticians we lived in a world of probability not possibility and they illustrated it like this...

If you were standing on one side of the barn and heard some hoof beats what would you expect to see? A Tibetan ox? A giraffe? A camel? An oryx?

Those are all possibilities but are any of them probabilities? No they are not. Don't be surprised to see a cow or horse come around the corner.

When we consider the testimony of nature we can clearly see that the earth had a beginning and has a complexity to it that cannot be duplicated by the smartest of humanity and cannot be reasonably explained by being an accident.

So as diagnosticians what do we conclude? There are a lot of possibilities but the probability is that the earth and all the life on it were created by an intelligent being. Are the Big Bang theory and specific evolution possibilities? Yes they are but they are not likely or probable.

It's then that we turn to the Bible record to find that intelligent being that was responsible for it all.

Someone told me one time that if you sat a monkey down in front of a typewriter and gave him enough time that eventually he could type out the Declaration of Independence. That's ridiculous...I know monkeys...they would tear the typewriter up and defecate all over it.

Don't waste your time and life chasing after every little possibility that exists. Follow after probabilities and keep your eyes open for the rare possibility that might pop up.

Examine nature carefully and carefully investigate the Holy Scriptures.

Veterinary

Wayward Members

Back when I was in large animal practice one of the issues we had to deal with were "Crypt" horses. Those are male horses with hormone producing tissue in their abdominal cavity. "Crypt" horses behave like Stallions and are barely manageable.

The treatment is surgery which has some risk involved. You can imagine laying down a 1000 lb. horse behind your clinic with less than perfect anesthesia and going in to find that hormone producing tissue. Clients usually ask if there is any risk involved. Yes, your horse might die. An old time veterinarian told me he would tell clients…"If he dies, you don't really have a horse anyway do you?"

Often in congregations we have those members who wander away from our services. As shepherds we have the responsibility to try to herd those sheep back to the flock. Usually that means a phone call or two, sending a card/note, texting, messaging on Facebook or trying to set up an appointment to go visit.

Many times those things don't work. As a last resort I try to just go knock on their door. Some people aren't comfortable with that and feel like it's an invasion of privacy or it just goes too far.

I know this, that God is going to hold me personally responsible for the sheep in our flock and I'd better have a good answer for Him when he asks me about what I did to take care of his sheep when I meet up with him on the Judgment Day.

Those wayward members may never respond to any of our efforts but let's try everything we can possibly do and if the "surgery" is a success then it's worth whatever risk it took. Because after all…we don't really have a horse any how do we.

Jokes

No Joke

There's an old joke about a farmer who was going broke farming so he quit and started selling hammers. He would buy hammers for $3 apiece and sell them for $2 each. He was happy and doing a pretty good business but a friend advised him that for every hammer he sold he was losing $1. His reply? "It's more profitable than farming."

That joke is similar to what people sometimes do with their lives. Activities like drunkenness, sexual immorality, unfaithfulness to a spouse, etc. can cause folks to view their lives as being spiritually bankrupt. So they decide to go to church or pray or read the Bible every once in a while without actually correcting the behaviors that got them into such a big mess to begin with.

Going to church, praying and reading the Bible are good things to do but until we take some corrective action in our lives and commit ourselves fully to Jesus Christ and his teachings, we are still "going broke"…Like buying hammers for $3 and selling them for $2.

Don't make a joke out of your lives.

Jokes

Flee Fornication

There's an old joke I love to tell about what the smallest sin in the Bible is. It falls flat on people with superficial Bible knowledge so I usually like to tell it to those who seem to have an in depth knowledge of the Bible…Preachers and church goers and such-like. Oh yeah, the punch line? "Flea fornication"…that is small, very small.

The reality is that the sin of fornication is huge in the Bible. It is constantly spoken against…much more than murder for instance. The reason? Because it is so prevalent in all generations of people.

Sexual intercourse is, of course, a very pleasurable activity. However, it has its greatest pleasure when it is set aside as a special thing, an intimacy that is reserved for a very special person…a spouse.

For some people sexual intercourse is like shaking hands…they'll shake hands with anyone and it becomes so common that it loses its true value. It even has different names to make it sound better like "we're together" and a "trial marriage". You can call it whatever you want to. God calls it fornication and punishes people for it.

Let fleas fornicate…the rest of us should flee from it.

Talking Frogs

There's an old guy at the gym where I work out…we'll call him Bosquez. Bosquez is great at telling jokes. His face is very expressive, he gives just enough detail and he has a slow, gravelly voice with a Hispanic accent. I love to watch him tell jokes. The trouble is, he doesn't know any good jokes. So I thought I would help him out with my "talking frog" joke. The condensed version goes like this…an old man playing golf comes across a talking frog who informs him that she is really a beautiful, young princess who has been placed under a curse. If the old guy will kiss her, she can transform back and they can be married and live happily ever after. The frog really has a hard time convincing the old guy to do this and finally the old guy explains…"I think I'd rather have a talking frog."

Most people really laugh at that joke…not Bosquez. Bosquez looks at me through those thick glasses and says…"Yeah, we just want someone to talk to." He never smiled.

In our day and time, and perhaps every day and time, most young men who are looking for a wife are looking for a young woman of beauty and sensuality. Certainly physical attraction is important but importance should also be placed on things like character and chastity and godliness. People can't help how they look but they can control…who they are…and the one who possesses inner beauty can be far more attractive than the one who possesses external beauty only.

According to Bosquez he's had a lot of girl friends and wives over his 78 year life span. Don't be like him and learn the hard way that a talking frog may be more attractive than a beautiful woman.

Managing Anger With Subjection

An old friend of mine told a joke that goes something like this…an older guy tells a younger guy, they're two theories about how to calm down an angry woman. The younger fellow quickly asks what are they? The older gent replies…it doesn't matter because neither one of them work (they're just unproven theories).

That's pretty funny, especially to men, but the truth is that anger is not gender specific…everybody gets angry…men and women. There may be a lot of "theories" about anger but the truth is that God's word has "factual" information about anger.

Here's a fact about controlling anger…subjection. It's hard to get into a "knock down drag out" if one of the parties is demonstrating subjection…which by the way is commanded of Christians (Ephesians 5:21).

So what does subjection look like? Consider Sarah and Abraham…

"For this is how the holy women of the past adorned themselves. They put their hope in God and were subject to their husbands, just as Sarah obeyed Abraham and called him lord. You are her children if you do what is right and refuse to quiver in fear."

Imagine if you were angry with your wife and had your dander up and were fixing to blow your fuse and she quietly got on her knees and bowed her head and said…"I'm sorry please forgive me (Lord)."

That will take the wind out of your sails and the good ship anger will come to a dead stop.

There's a lot of theories and advice your un-godly friends might give you about how to handle anger, but if anger is a problem in any of your relationships you might want to listen to God.

Parenting

Socialization

One of the things I see in kids of all ages is the behavior of being uncomfortable or even terrified of social situations.

Let me explain it like this. In our business we deal with all kinds of dog owners. Most of them give great care to their dogs. Some of those dogs when they come into our office are terrified and that terror can be manifested by behaviors as mild as trembling or as severe as aggression (fear biters).

These dogs are not abused, far from it, they get the best of care. The problem is they have received either poor or no socialization training. Those dogs invariably never see anything but their own back yards and when faced with a social situation they have not experienced before they become terrified.

The same thing happens with kids, they are fed well and in every way taken good care of but they are not encouraged to experience social situations. They don't know how to interact with adults, they haven't been trained in common basic courtesies such as greeting someone with a handshake, making eye contact and interactive social conversation.

Parents should encourage, train and seek opportunities for their children to engage in social interaction.

In my office owners not only bring their pet in but also their children. Frequently those kids are playing some handheld video game. That's disrespectful to me and a disservice to them. Make them put those games away and pay attention. Make them shake my hand and speak to me. Show me some signs of respect.

When I was in the sixth grade my parents encouraged me to walk the neighborhood with our lawnmower, knock on doors and seek lawn mowing jobs...three dollars a yard as I recall. From the time I was in the eighth until the eleventh grade, I threw newspapers and at the end of the month had to knock on my customer's doors to collect my wages.

I had to engage in those activities because my parents did not lavish money or the things money can buy on me or my brothers. They taught us how to work and how to interact with adults.

Dog owners can give great care to their pets; proper food, proper medical care, play time and discipline. And yet these pets can soil a veterinarian's office and bite the people who are trying to help it.

Socialize your dogs and your kids. Keep me from getting bit and help your kids excel in life.

Respect or Anger?

There is some Bible evidence for the idea that the most important thing you can teach your children is…respect.

Number five of the 10 Commandments commands children to respect their parents. The first four commandments deal with God, the rest of the commandments deal with how we interact with others and of those commandments, respecting one's parents is numero uno.

How important is the command? Children who violated it were to be put to death.

So, arguably, the most important thing you can do for a child is to teach him respect. Teach a child respect and God will bless him and you. Fail to teach him respect and God will curse that child in life and in death. A rebellious child causes great misery to parents.

Parents have the ability to teach a child respect and also have the ability to teach a child anger and rebellion.

How do you teach a child to be angry? Be a poor example. Make one set of rules for a child and a different set of rules for yourself. Sit in front of the TV every night and drink beer and ignore your family. Be selfish, always think of yourself first. Over punish the kid for minor infractions. Show preferential treatment between your kids…call one smart and the other one stupid. Do what ever you can to always criticize and never praise or encourage your kids.

Do these things and you will have earned for yourself a miserable life and a seat on the front row in hell and you likely will have driven your child to hell.

Work at training your child respect and things will be…well.

Parenting

How to Work

I work a lot of kids from time to time. Some kids aren't used to working and need supervision. Sometimes I give a job to do and when I get back the bare minimum has been done. Usually that has to do with how well the parents have trained them. I worked a kid last week whose family owns a ranch. He is used to building fence and really a lot of labor intensive work. Zach was working at the clinic last week and we needed a tool so I sent him to my house to get it. When he got back I noticed there were about six tools in the back of my truck. Later we needed to air up a tire on a wheelbarrow so I sent him back for my portable air compressor. When I checked on him later I didn't see my air compressor...I saw my other wheelbarrow.

The best kind of workers are those who don't need supervision and those who look ahead and try to anticipate what we might need next. I like workers who do not just follow orders but who also try to understand the job and make meaningful suggestions. The Lord's work is a lot like that. The Lord gives us work to do and really not much supervision...we'll give account of ourselves at the end of the job. To those who work hard he will bless with more ability and responsibility...make them better, more efficient workers. As a loving Father he realizes we may make mistakes in our labors, and I think overlook those mistakes. The one mistake he won't overlook is...not trying. Read the parable of the talents in Matthew 25. What kind of worker are you?

Doc Mayfield told me that his dad was a plumber and when he was a kid his dad told him to dig a trench that had a quarter inch drop every foot. I think Doc was 10 or 11 at the time. When Doc's dad got back and saw Doc just sitting around and the job not done...he didn't say one word...he just got his belt out and whipped the tar out of him. When he came back the next time the job was done. Doc says he loved that old man.

Scatter Shooting While Thinking About Parenting

Families are a lot different today, a lot of married couples wait until later in life to have children and then they only have a few kids. In the old days, couples married at a younger age and had more children. Fathers often worked two jobs to support their families. There wasn't a lot of time to consider "innovative" parenting techniques…a belt/switch was quicker and required less thought.

When my uncle Alton was 12 or 13 he came home from school with a homemade tattoo. My grandfather sat him down and removed it with a pocketknife. I'm sure he didn't anticipate that when he was getting the thing.

When Walker was a kid I worked two out of three Saturdays. So the Saturday I was off I always had some plan to get something done around the house. Often times I was foiled by Walker having some friend over to spend the night. I made a rule that if a friend was coming over he had to work too. The friends always seemed to enjoy it.

When kids knock on the door selling something I always try to buy it, no matter how worthless it is, because it takes a lot of courage for a kid to knock on a stranger's door and make a sales pitch. They say that positive reinforcement is a much stronger teaching tool than negative reinforcement.

Parents are supposed to teach children to be good workers. It seems to me that nowadays we're teaching them to be good beggars. As a business owner we're always being hit up for "sponsorships" for little league teams or camps or whatever. Frequently it's not even the kid making the request…it's the parents. My office manager said the other day, "what's up with giving money to cheer leaders…don't they know how to wash cars anymore?"

When my uncle CB was 8 or 9, my grandmother took him to see the Navy dentist for a bad tooth. They waited in line for a long time and when they finally got in to see the dentist CB threw a big fit and grandma told the dentist never mind and took him home. When she got him home she sat on him and pulled out his tooth with a pair of pliers. Never underestimate the power of a Navy wife.

Some kids knocked on my door one day selling candy bars for some school function. I didn't really need any more candy bars so I told them I would pay them $20 if they weeded my flower bed. Their mom gave them permission and we both received something of value. Selling candy bars is the first cousin of begging.

Every semester I would ask Walker if he wanted to go to school. He would answer in the affirmative and I would pay for it. He never made very many passing grades. So one semester I asked him if he wanted to go to school. He said yes and I told him about the new plan; he would pay for school and I would reimburse him for every passing grade. I don't think I was out very much money that semester. After he got married he graduated Magna Cum Laude. His wife swung a bigger hammer than I did.

My business partner had three brothers and was one of 9 kids. When his dad would send them to the barber shop in Kingsville, Texas they were always very careful to tell the barber how they wanted their hair cut but they always received the exact same haircut. They found out later that their dad would call the barber ahead of time and say "I don't care what those boys say, this is how I want you to cut their hair…"

When I was in the fourth grade I had a friend who lived across the street who always picked on me. After several complaints to my mother she finally told me, "I want you to fight that kid and if you don't I'm going to give you a whipping." I still remember the fight. Somehow we continued to be friends. Years later I asked the 6.0 version of my mother and she said, "Well…that kid was a bully."

Our dad had rules for me and my two brothers about how to hit each other. We couldn't hit each other in the face, belly or back. Dad said we could hit each other in the shoulder area. Dad didn't encourage us to hit each other he just knew the realities of raising three boys and tried to manage it.

Mom and Dad didn't care too much about grades when we were growing up. As long as we passed we were OK. My report cards were heavy on "C's" and light on "A's". Somehow we did OK; I'm a veterinarian, Scott is a dentist and Greg is a mechanical engineer. Still, I always pushed my kids to make good grades. I guess the acorn fell off the tree and rolled into a river on that one.

My kids still laugh about Saturday mornings at our house. Sometimes I would line them up and with buckets in one hand and shovels in the other we would scour one acre for grass bur plants. I'm glad I could create such pleasant memories.

Bible Study

Doctors, Preachers, and Other Specialists

I finished a book recently that describes why doctors think the way they do. One of the things illustrated was that general practitioners had a tendency to accept whatever diagnosis that a specialist makes because they are board certified specialists...experts if you will. The problem is that specialists tend to be wrong 20% of the time.

I think a similar problem can exist among preachers, teachers and Christians in general. We have a tendency to accept the teachings of our own heroes of faith as being infallible: perhaps a preacher whose tutelage we grew up under or a noted gospel meeting preacher or maybe a preacher who wrote a book. Going back further...maybe someone who taught during the so called "issues" of the 1950s or even someone who taught during the restoration movement, etc.

In a medical condition a wrong diagnosis can lead to a lifetime of the wrong medications, continued poor health and maybe even death.

What if our great heroes of faith were wrong 20% of the time? How would that affect our spiritual health?

Study God's word continuously. Pray to God for spiritual enlightenment. Don't be afraid to listen to opposing views and don't be afraid to change your mind.

Listen to your doctor but don't be afraid to get a second, third or however many opinions you might need for your physical health and remember that your spiritual health is much more important than your physical health.

Intellectual Dishonesty

Congregations are shaped by their teachers and preachers. Since most congregations have just one preacher then he has a tremendous shaping effect on the congregation where he preaches.

If that preacher is intellectually dishonest then the congregation has a tendency to be composed of those who have a low scriptural IQ or those who are apathetic towards the scriptures. Those who have a high spiritual IQ or who truly care about God's word won't tolerate intellectual dishonesty and will look for another church.

Examples of intellectual dishonesty would include agenda based teaching. That is…having an opinion about something and gathering and massaging scriptures to support that opinion.

Here's another…if there is a scriptural dilemma and both sides have merit, only present the side you agree with and ignore the other view.

When I was a young Christian (and had a low scriptural IQ) I would listen to the preachers and teachers and take their arguments and go out and wage war with the denominations. Some of the time, the arguments were leaky and wouldn't hold water and I would stand there looking like a spiritual idiot holding an empty bucket. That's because I was shaped by someone who was intellectually dishonest or scripturally naïve themselves.

The goal for congregations should be to honestly examine the scriptures and to encourage those with different views to speak up so those views can be considered. Otherwise we might end up with a congregation that is spiritually inbred and that ends up with severe and crippling spiritual defects and handicaps.

Introductions and Conclusions

Introductions and conclusions in a letter are generally short summations of what is contained in the letter. A conclusion is usually a restatement of the introduction.

Compare the introduction and conclusion in the Roman letter…for instance.

In Romans 1:11, Paul wants to help "establish" the Roman Christians ; the same thing in the conclusion (Romans 16:25) "Now to him that is able to establish you…"

In Romans 1:2, "the Gospel which he promised through "his prophets in the Holy Scriptures." In Romans 16:25, "my gospel…now manifested…by the Scriptures of the prophets."

In Romans 1:5, "unto obedience of faith among all the nations". In Romans 16:26, "made known unto all the nations unto obedience of faith".

See the similarities?

So from the introduction and conclusion (which agree with each other) we can say that the part in between is an expansion of the introduction and conclusion.

Specifically then the letter to the Romans is about being established in the Gospel through the preaching about Jesus Christ and the obedience of faith. It is for all nations, as has been revealed by the prophets in the scriptures. To God be the glory.

Bible Study

Interpreting Scripture: Understand Purpose

When interpreting a passage of Scripture it's always best to have some understanding about the purpose of what's being written.

For instance in 1 John 5:1, "Whosoever believes that Jesus is the Christ is born of God…"

OK, without giving some consideration to why the letter was written we might conclude that anyone who believes that Jesus is the Christ is born of God and the only thing we have to do is believe. Boom…. I believe, therefore I am born of God and have a one way ticket to , heaven.

That would be a wrong conclusion for several reasons.

1 John was written because there were Christians teaching that Jesus was not the Christ. They started with an incorrect premise. They reasoned that since all human flesh is sinful and deity cannot have anything to do with sin that deity could not dwell in a human body. Therefore Jesus had no deity in him…he was not the Christ.

Ok so knowing that…let's interpret the verse again. Whoever believes that deity indwells within Jesus is born of God. Those who do not believe that Jesus is the Christ are not born of God and are false teachers and false believers.

So the belief in this passage is used to contrast the belief of Christians with the Anti-Christians.

So you see the importance of understanding why a scripture was written and to not make some hasty application that might have disastrous consequences. After all Satan and his minions believed correctly that Jesus was the Christ but they were not "born of God" were they?

The Old Testament in Romans

I find it interesting that the letter to the Romans contains more than 60 quotations from the Old Testament. That is interesting because the majority of Christians in Rome were from a non-Jewish back ground. And yet Paul makes extensive use of the Old Testament to a people who were totally ignorant of the Old Testament before they were introduced to Jesus Christ.

For comparisons sake we usually say that the Gospel of Matthew was written to a Jewish audience because it contains 64 references to the Old Testament. That makes sense because the Jews knew the Old Testament.

I submit to you that the reason Paul used so many references from the Old Testament to the Roman Christians was because they were very familiar with it…they were converted to Christianity through the teaching of the Old Testament. In fact, when the gospel is referenced in Romans 1:16 it is referencing the gospel (or good news of salvation) revealed in the Old Testament.

The "righteousness of God" (Romans 1:17) that is revealed from "faith unto faith" is revealed in the Old Testament as God dealt righteously with faithful men like Abraham, Isaac, Moses, David, etc.

The "wrath of God" (Romans 1:18) that is "revealed from heaven" is revealed in the Old Testament as God dealt with righteous wrath against Sodom and Gomorrah, Egypt, the destruction of Jerusalem, etc.

Paul uses over 60 quotations from the Old Testament when he writes the Roman Christians because they had been taught extensively in it. The stories of the Old Testament were their stories, the heroes of the Old Testament were their heroes. Abraham was their father and Sarah was their mother.

Sometimes, in my opinion, we over emphasize the New Testament and under emphasize the Old Testament and relegate it to children's classes. To do so would be a mistake. After all, the faith of the Romans that was famous world-wide was based upon the teachings concerning the good news of salvation found in the Old Testament.

Prayer

Preparation for Prayer

I don't know about you but I don't pray very well unless I have prepared myself for prayer...both in private and public prayer. Personally, I don't like to open worship services with a prayer. I like to pray a little deeper into the service when I have had time to sing a few songs and reflect on the words, and the needs of my brothers and sisters in Christ, etc.

Also, in private prayer if I think "oh I need to pray" and start praying then those prayers tend to be short and routine. If I can begin my day by reading from God's word or by reflecting on my blessings or problems then my prayers have more depth to them.

Holy people of old prepared themselves for prayer by fasting and wearing humble clothing.

Prayer is important but not just praying for the sake of praying. Prepare yourselves for prayer. I've got a feeling that God doesn't want to hear prayers recited from memory but rather prayers generated from the heart.

The Days of Our Lives

As human beings we understand that we have a limited number of days to live upon this earth. As servants (employees) of God we understand that those days should be spent working for God. So at the beginning of a new day an assessment should be made about how we performed for God on the previous day and a plan should be made for the new day.

The previous day's assessment should include; did I actively violate any of God's commandments, i.e. did I sin? The assessment should also include some thought about the casual social interaction we have with other people. In my social interaction did I represent my employer (God) in a positive way? Was I kind, helpful, encouraging etc. In addition, how did I do in my planned social interaction? Which brings us to this…planning the new day.

Since we have a finite number of days on earth, each one of them is precious and should be devoted in some form or fashion to the Lord. For example, today I'm going to visit someone who is lonely, a home bound widow, a sick person, etc. Today I'm going to encourage someone who is neglecting their abilities. Today I'm going to repair a broken relationship. Today I'm going to interact and get to know someone at church who I only know on a handshake basis (a handshake friend). Today I'm going to help a poor person.

Things are done by littles and as those little things that we do day by day build up they become a huge monument to God. Plan and assess your days or otherwise you may wake up at the end of your life and realize you've only accumulated a bunch of wasted days.

Surprised By Prayer

A transformation has occurred in my prayer life, one that I didn't predict or expect and I don't really know when it happened but it's real. It dawned on me tonight when I was sitting in on a Bible class about prayer and our attitude about prayer.

I guess prayer for me has been an obligatory sort of thing...a measure of faith as a Christian. I am a Christian therefore I pray.

Tonight I realized that I love my "hour" of prayer and look forward to it. In fact, if somehow something interferes with it...I am deeply annoyed.

You see for some time now I get up in the morning and sit down with my Bible and read it. After I am done reading I get down on my knees and pray.

Sometimes I pray about things that are bothering me...like an issue with someone or something and I tell God that my spirit is troubled and I'm not sure what to do and to please help me. Let me tell you this God has helped me 100% of the time with those situations and of course I always thank him.

I thank God for Julie and ask him that we might have a long life together and that we would die on the exact same day.

I thank God for our family and my mother and Julie's mother.

I thank God for our children and their excellent mates.

I thank God for my grandchildren and ask him to protect them.

I pray that my family members that need it would find faith.

I pray for the old folks at church that I love so much.

I pray for the special needs of the congregation that I am a shepherd of.

I thank God for that morning's reading.

I pray that God would open my eyes so I might understand the truths he has recorded for me.

I pray to God that he would help me write articles and that I may become a better teacher.

I thank God for my prosperity and my good health.

And I pray that God would use me to influence others to become faithful.

I love my "hour of prayer" that doesn't quite last an hour. If something happens and I need to talk to God I impatiently wait for that special time I have with him.

I was reading in Deuteronomy this morning that Israel had to "tithe" in order to learn to revere God. I suspect the same thing is true with prayer…you start praying because you are commanded to and then wake up one day and realize that God is not just some made up story but a true and real friend that you can't do without.

Reasons Why God Doesn't Answer Prayer (James 4:3)

A mistake Bible students sometimes make is to read a passage superficially or fail to consider other relevant passages and make inappropriate applications.

Take 1 John 5:14, for example…"This is the confidence we have in approaching God: that if we ask anything according to his will, he hears us."

A superficial reading might lead one to believe that we can pray for "anything" and fail to consider that the "anything" is modified by "according to his will."

That's why you see people praying for things like winning the lottery or that a boy or girl might "like" them or for one's favorite sports team to win or for someone we don't like to suffer misfortune.

This type of prayer reflects poor Bible study.

Consider James 4:3 "When you ask, you do not receive, because you ask with wrong motives, that you may spend what you get on your pleasures."

It is not "according to God's will" that we pray for things that are self-serving. It is "according to his will" to pray for the necessities and not the extravagances of life.

It's important that we become good Bible students so that we can make the proper applications of God's word. God will not answer silly prayers and I suspect is insulted by them. Let's make God proud of us in our prayer lives.

Spiritual Arrogance

Luke 18: 9–14 records two prayers: a self-righteous prayer and a self-critical prayer. The two men were praying in the same place and at the same time. The one thanked God that he was not evil like other people and recounted to God the good things that he had done in his life. The other asked God for mercy for his short comings.

Here's the thing…we have all done some good in our lives and it would be easy to make a list of those things and carefully recite them to God. Almost as if God didn't know those things already and needed to be reminded.

The best approach is to have a short term memory of the good things we have done and to have a heightened sensitivity about our short comings and our need to be more Christ-like. Let's face it, if we were in a contest with Jesus Christ and trying to best him with our good works we would come in second…every time. Realizing that let's be truthful and self-critical in our prayers. The self-critical man went home "justified before God."

Esther

UNCLE ROB'S BLOG

A Few Thoughts About The Book Of Esther

- When King Ahasuerus commanded Queen Vashti to attend his banquet wearing her crown to display her great beauty, he was entirely within his rights as a king and a husband. It was a state function and she was to attend in her capacity as a queen (wearing her crown).

- There is nothing in the text that even suggests there was anything improper in his command.

- Queen Vashti ignored an official request made before a multitude of people at an official banquet. Her behavior could not be ignored.

- Queen Vashti's refusal to appear is in stark contrast to Queen Esther's reluctance to appear before King Ahasuerus. At one point, Queen Esther had not seen her husband in 30 days because he had not asked for her.

- Haman, the king's second in command, had a plot to exterminate all the Jews. If Queen Vashti were still queen he would have had no opposition.

- God dethroned Queen Vashti and elevated Esther to take her place as queen and protect his people.

- Esther and her fellow Jews were Jews who decided to stay in Persia and not be repatriated to Judea.

- One lesson from the Book of Esther is that God protects his people wherever they are. Even if they decide to stay in a foreign land.

- How many wives and concubines did King Ahasuerus have? Who knows? King Solomon had 1000 wives and 300 concubines.

- Now we see why King Ahasuerus made it a crime punishable by death to approach him in his inner court uninvited. If you have

Esther

over a thousand women and their children in your harem you might like some alone time.

- King Ahasuerus was about 36 years old when he became king, 39 years old when Vashti ignored his command and 43 years old when he married Esther. The time spent between Vashti and Esther was four years. Ahasuerus was busy invading Greece during this time. Ahasuerus and Esther had been married about 5 years when Haman plotted to kill all the Jews.

- Esther was not involved in a beauty contest where there is one winner and everyone else goes home. They were all concubines of the king except Esther who was wife and queen. They would live the rest of their lives in the king's harem.

Esther was a willing participant in the queen contest.

The Book Of Esther

The selection of Esther as queen of the Persian Empire has sometimes been characterized as a "beauty contest"...which in my mind is a complete mischaracterization of the event.

When King Ahasuerus decided he needed a new queen he had young virgins selected from all 127 provinces in his kingdom ranging from Ethiopia to India. If just one young woman from each province was selected, that's 127 young virgin women. At the time of their gathering they were placed in the "first harem" and were considered to be concubines/wives of the king. Unlike a beauty contest there would be no going home for these young women. One of them would become queen but they would all be concubines/wives.

There was a 12 month education/beautification process involving cosmetics, choice food, oil of myrrh and spices before the selection would be made. The interview for the queenship was a personal one with the king himself. Esther was not an unwilling participant in this process. When it was Esther's turn, she went to King Ahasuerus' palace in the evening and spent the night with him and was taken to a new harem the next morning...the second harem. No longer a virgin she had consummated her marriage to King Ahasuerus and in the process won his favor and became queen of the Persian Empire.

Esther could have been quite young at the time, perhaps as young as 14 years, and now she was the second most important person on the royal side of the kingdom. Her older cousin Mordecai, who had been her guardian, would become the second most important person on the political side of the kingdom. For me, the story of Mordecai is more important than the story of Esther. In fact, the book could easily be named the Book of Mordecai. Amazing that God would place two Jews in such high places in a world empire...more on Mordecai next week.

Esther

A Great Hero

Every great hero is born of great necessity and great adversity. Mordecai the Jew faced great necessity...the threat of the annihilation of his people, and a great adversary...Haman the Agagite.

Haman was second in command of the great Persian Empire. He carried King Ahasuerus' signet ring which carried the authority of the king. Haman was informed that Mordecai refused to bow and pay homage as Haman entered through the king's gate. He was also informed that Mordecai was a Jew.

Instead of reserving punishment for Mordecai alone Haman devised a scheme to punish all the Jews. He schemed and "cast the lot" (astrology) and got King Ahasuerus to agree to issue an edict that all the Jews in the entire kingdom, which stretched from India to Ethiopia, could be "destroyed, killed and annihilated" including "young and old, and women and children" on the 13th day of the month of Adar.

Seems a little excessive doesn't it? Every word in the Bible means something and the word, "Agagite", is huge in the understanding of Haman. An Agagite is a descendant of King Agag who was king of the Amalekites. The Amalekites were a people who, centuries before, God had ordered the Jews to annihilate. Undoubtedly Haman knew this and now he was in a position to do something about it. To do to the Jews what the Jews had done to his people.

In comparison to Haman, Mordecai the Jew appeared to be a nobody, but to God he was a somebody, a simple man of faith selected by God to overcome a great adversary so that God's people could be preserved.

Mordecai the Magnificent

Mordecai was a man of responsibility.

- ◆ When Esther was orphaned he took her in "as his own daughter."

Mordecai was a man of advice.

- ◆ He instructed Esther not to reveal her nationality…she was a Jew.

Mordecai cared about Esther.

- ◆ He walked "back and forth" every day outside the harem where Esther was kept, to learn "how Esther was and how she fared."
- ◆ After Esther was made queen he sat outside the king's gate.

Mordecai was loyal to King Ahasuerus and the Persian Empire.

- ◆ He obeyed the command to bring Esther to become a wife of the king.
- ◆ He became aware of a plot to assassinate the king and made it known. The conspirators were hanged and Mordecai's name was recorded in the "Book of Chronicles."

Mordecai was loyal to God.

- ◆ He refused to bow down and pay homage to Haman. Even after Haman devised and implemented a plan to annihilate the Jews Mordecai still refused to pay homage to him.
- ◆ Mordecai made a public display in the middle of the city in "sackcloth and ashes…wailing loud and bitterly," when Haman's plan to annihilate the Jews was made public. By doing so he announced his loyalty to God as a Jew.

Mordecai planned and made provision to thwart Haman.

- ◆ He prepared by acquiring a copy of the edict and finding out the "exact amount of money Haman had promised to the king."
- ◆ He equipped Esther with this information.
- ◆ He managed Esther's concerns about approaching King Ahasuerus.

Mordecai's actions caused many people to convert to Judaism because of the "dread of the Jews." While Haman was alive no one wanted to be a Jew…with Mordecai's rise to power it was cool to be a Jew.

Mordecai was politically wise.

- ◆ Even though King Ahasuerus had authorized the Jews to "annihilate the entire army of any people or province that might attack them" and to "plunder them." The Jews did not take any "plunder." Why? Because "plundering" was not their motivation and Mordecai did not want it to be charged against them.

Mordecai instituted an annual celebration for the Jews to commemorate their great victory…Purim.

Mordecai was a man of great faith (obviously), that is made abundantly clear in his conversation with the reluctant Queen Esther when he told her,

"For if you remain silent at this time, relief and deliverance will arise from the Jews from another place and you and your father's house will perish."

Mordecai placed all his hope not on Esther but on God. Mordecai's name is recorded 55 times in the book of Esther. Esther's name is recorded 54 times. They were both important to the story. Esther was not just a pretty face, she was wise and faithful as well. More on her next week.

Marriage

Marriage 101

Most young people contemplating marriage anticipate a lifetime commitment with a loved one and the blessing of children and grandchildren. Unfortunately, that doesn't always work out.

The recipe for happiness and longevity in marriage is found in the Scriptures. It begins with a young woman and a young man who are sexually pure. They respect God's laws regarding marriage and make iron clad vows to each other and to God. Those vows are witnessed by family and friends who serve to make the young couple accountable to their vows. It's like a little plant that needs a little watering, a little weeding, a little protection and a little sunshine so that in time it can grow into a strong and beautiful tree.

There is a new method that young couples commonly employ today to reach the goal of successful marriage. They live together for a while in a relationship that mimics marriage sans vows. The goal, I suppose, is to see if the relationship will work and if it does then take vows or let the relationship evolve into a common law marriage. Like a little sickly plant that someone plants and ignores and says, "let's see if it grows."

There are two reasons why this is the wrong approach; a moral one and a practical one. First of all God forbids sex outside the marital relationship. It's wrong.

Secondly, as a practical matter, there is no accountability in such a relationship. At the first sign of trouble in the "living together" relationship the unhappy mate can conclude this isn't working and bail out. Let's face it, all marriages have problems but mates who have vowed vows and are held accountable by their family and friends tend to work through their problems and the marriage grows stronger.

Julie and I never considered living together outside the bounds of marriage. Our families would have thrown a fit. I would have had the combined weight of grandparents, uncles and aunts, and people that I hold the dearest in the world raining down on me.

In addition, if we had "lived together" we would probably not be together now. We have had our share of troubles in our marriage and without vows we might have separated and become entangled in some other relationship destroying any hope of reconciliation.

If you want to have a long happy marriage…trust God and not your ungodly friends.

UNCLE ROB'S BLOG

45th Wedding Anniversary

This is something I posted to Facebook on June 1st. Happy anniversary to my wife of 45 years. (We were married in 1973.) 45 years ago today, one week after graduating from high school, we eloped to Lake Charles, Louisiana. I tell people the reason we did that is because at the time…in Texas…they wouldn't let first cousins marry. But they would in Louisiana. Of course that's a joke. Julie Bedwell is the only girl I ever dated. A lot of people would say that we somehow found our soul mates as if failures in marriage are somehow due to bad luck. The truth is that we were committed to each other based on our faith in Jesus Christ and would not allow Satan to separate what God had put together. God has blessed me in many ways but my greatest blessing has been Julie Perkins.

Happiness and Sorrow

Julie and I were at a gathering last night and I saw an older couple (probably married 50 plus years) who I know on a casual basis. A friend told me that the wife had gone into the hospital for a cardiac procedure and had nearly died. He added that he was pretty sure she would pull through but he wasn't sure her husband would. My friend told me the man was so shaken and overcome with worry for his wife that he couldn't even talk.

I watched the older couple and while everyone else was gathered around tables, playing games and having fun…they sat off by themselves just holding hands and looking at each other and saying a few words to each other and smiling at each other.

And I thought I saw in him happiness and sorrow. Happiness that the thing he treasured the most in this world, his wife, had been given back to him and sorrow that it was just a preview of what was to come.

It was a learning moment for me that things don't last forever and to treasure the moments with each other and perhaps be a little more patient with each other.

There are a lot of great things in this life but unfortunately a lot of sorrow too. Thank God there is something better waiting for those who believe in Jesus Christ.

UNCLE ROB'S BLOG

My Husband Doesn't Love Me

Imagine you were at a dance and you saw a girl on the other side of the dance floor that just...took your breath away...her eyes sparkled, she smiled at you and you thought she was the prettiest thing you had ever seen and were summoning up the courage to ask her to dance when your dad came up and said, "I want you to dance with that other girl that no one else is paying attention to." You looked over and saw a plain homely kind of a girl and your heart sank but you did it and danced the whole night with her. Finally at the very end you got to dance with the girl of your dreams and your heart beat so hard you thought it was going to break out of your chest.

That's kind of like the story of Jacob, Leah and Rachel in the book of Genesis. Jacob had his heart set on Rachel but God had other plans for him and he had to marry Leah first in order to also marry her sister Rachel.

Here's the thing...Leah knew Jacob didn't love her. Jacob only had eyes for Rachel. What do you do when you realize your husband doesn't love you? With many tears Leah prayed to God and God heard her prayers and opened her womb and gave her six sons and one daughter whom Jacob loved with all his heart...and Rachel? God closed her womb so she could feel some of Leah's hurt.

When I used to work cattle every so often we would push a Brahma (Bramer) through the chute. Often times they would go down in the chute and "sull," stopping the whole process. You could put a kink in their tails or hit them with a Hot Shot but you just couldn't get them to move until they were ready. [sull – refusing to move.]

Leah didn't "sull;" she did what she could do, gave it a little time and left the rest up to God. Rachel eventually had two boys but died during the birth of the second. Leah lived a long life with Jacob and felt his love and was buried by his side. God does answer the prayers of his faithful ones (including Rachel).

Don't despair if you're not the prettiest one at the dance. God knows who you are and like Leah can make your offspring as numerous as the sand on the beach...one of whom was Jesus Christ. Have a little faith.

God Hates Divorce

Malachi 2:10–12 reveals to us that God hates divorce. That's not like me hating beets. I do hate beets and refuse to eat them but when God hates something he goes a step further...he punishes the beets (so to speak).

Malachi reveals that the people were weeping and wailing because God didn't pay attention to their prayers or favor them with blessings. They were perplexed because God was not being a "God" to them.

The reason for this was because God was a witness when marriage vows were exchanged and they were breaking their vows and divorcing each other. God is faithful as a witness.

Something that is lost in wedding ceremonies today is the fact that the guests are there to witness vows and hold the married couple accountable to their vows so that when the day comes when a young couple is considering divorcing and breaking their vows the human witnesses can remind them of what was done and said on their wedding day.

God is faithful and accountable as a witness...he punishes people when they divorce. Their lives are not full of blessings.

I hate beets and won't eat them but I don't go out and find a field of beets and hoe them down. If God hated beets that's what he would do. Honor your vows. Don't divorce so you won't end up like a field of hoed up beets.

Wild Cattle and Wild Husbands

The peak period for cattle drives from South Texas to the rail heads in Kansas was in the 1870s. The vaquero/cowboys of South Texas would chase down and rope wild cattle in the brush to build a herd. Usually they had to tie off those wild cattle to mesquite trees and then let them choke down a little until they could be managed.

One of their tools was to take domesticated oxen…steers that had been trained to pull wagons, etc. frequently weighing 2500 pounds or so. The vaqueros would hobble their oxen to those wild steers and turn them loose. Eventually the ox would pull the steer home because they were used to being fed grain corn twice a day…and really liked it.

That concept reminds me of this verse…

"In the same way you wives must submit yourselves to your husbands, so that if any of them do not believe God's word, your conduct will win them over to believe. It will not be necessary for you to say a word" (1 Peter 3:1).

Now I'm not saying that a wife is an ox or that a husband is a wild steer but what I am saying is that sometimes husbands have certain notions that they need to be trained out of and it doesn't do any good at all for a wife to continually harp on those notions. The text says that a godly woman can change her husband not by words but by behavior.

By definition that means it's going to be a time consuming process that requires "patience in well doing."

You can imagine that 2500 pound ox hobbled to a 1000 pound steer slowly pulling that beast back to the ranch house where the steer finds out that a diet of corn is actually tastier than just eating grass and mesquite beans.

All I've got to say to you wives is keep pulling…you have the advantage because God is on your side and that wild untamed husband of yours will thank you one day (unless you ship him to the railheads in Kansas to be slaughtered…LOL).

Marriage

A Glorious Wife

There's a concept that is sometimes missed in Ephesians 5:22–33 which compares the church's relationship to Christ with the wife's relationship to her husband.

To paraphrase, Christ offered a conditional relationship to those who would believe in him. If believers would subject themselves in all things to his headship unconditionally he would accept them as his bride and love them in all things...unconditionally. His love would include giving up everything for them...ultimately his life (and everything in between). He had a purpose in this...he wanted "a glorious church (bride) without spot or wrinkle or any such thing; but that it should be holy and without blemish."

Sometimes we see stormy marital relationships where the husband wakes up one day and comes to the conclusion that he doesn't love his wife anymore, in fact he doesn't even like her. She's not the kind of wife he wants. Whose fault is that...hers? Maybe...but maybe it's his fault.

If Ephesians teaches anything it teaches that Christ did some things to prepare a glorious church for himself. Some husbands want to just walk into headship without paying a price...without doing anything to demonstrate love for their wives. When the reality is that if she could see demonstrable love she might be a glorious wife and accept his headship.

So husbands if you ever get the feeling that you don't like your wife anymore...it may not be her fault. She is what you made her.

Full-grown Christians understand this concept. They have subtracted pride from their lives and replaced it with humility and appreciation (and headship) for the ones with whom they have mated with for life.

Funerals

UNCLE ROB'S BLOG

Emilio Sanchez Funeral

We were able to go to the viewing for Emilio and his funeral. The viewing was more emotional…Tabby and Trey both got up and said some things about their Dad. Of course, we dismissed services at the building on Wednesday evening and had our service at the funeral home. Walker led singing and David had some very fine scripturally based things to say about Emilio. If we had kept the service at the building that would have been like studying the theory of Christianity…By having it at the funeral home it was more like practicing Christianity, i.e., comforting some of our grieving members.

Most of you know that the Sanchez family had been through some trying times. Emilio and Liz divorced and both remarried. Emilio divorced his second wife about the time he was diagnosed with cancer. From that moment in time Liz took over primary care of Emilio. After all she said Emilio was the father of her children. She either took him to the doctors, to MD Anderson or to San Antonio for treatment or she recruited people to do it for her. She made sure he was eating right and made sure he was taking his medications. She even moved him into the apartment complex she managed so he could be closer to receive better care. All of this with the consent of her second husband…Such incredible people.

I got to visit Emilio some but David Smitherman did more. During the last six months of his life Emilio was penitent and worked to repair the damage to God and to his family. I'm convinced that he's with God even now.

I was impressed with all the cops at the funeral. I'll bet there were about 150–200. Many of them filed down the aisle and one after another paid their respects at the coffin and then to the family. All dressed in their dress uniforms with their side arms on their belts…. Somber faced working men…a brotherhood of cops. Our Christian-hood was there as well, soldiers of Christ paying our last respects to our fellow soldier in Christ and to his family…our family.

Remember Emilio and don't forget to care and comfort for his children…Trey and Tabby.

Funerals

I'll never forget Emilio because we share a day...Nov 17 the day he was reborn is also my birthday. God bless you Emilio.

Glenn Torno Funeral

I went to Glenn Torno's funeral the other day. I try to make every funeral of church members and their families that I can. It was pretty easy to attend this funeral. Glenn attended at Borden Street Church of Christ in Sinton, Texas. I had come to know him on a casual basis because of my relationship with his family. When we first moved to Corpus Christi in 1982 we met Ray and Linda Torno. Our kids grew up with their kids. Of course Glen's other son Tim was at Parkway too but I had known him since college days.

Even before I met Glen I felt like I knew him because I knew his sons. Anyone who raised godly men like Ray and Tim must also be godly.

When I first met Glenn I sensed we had something in common... Glenn liked people. He was very gregarious and welcoming and Julie and I were even invited into their home. I was impressed.

I was also impressed to learn things about Glenn. Things like when he was 14 years old during the Depression he would drive a truck across the state delivering pipe. Farm raised kids aren't like city raised kids. I also learned that he set the 440 record in track and field at Sinton High School. That record lasted until 1964 when his son Ray broke it.

I really enjoyed hearing what Keith Miller his oldest grandson had to say. Keith and his Paw Paw would leave Sinton in Glen's old truck and his Paw Paw would start a story and that story wouldn't end until they pulled up into the driveway in Bayside 30 minutes later. As a kid he used to be so bored with those stories. As an adult he wishes that he could hear them one more time. Keith said they would drive around looking at the cotton fields. As a kid he thought... all these cotton fields look alike. As an adult he wished he could just drive with his Paw Paw just one more time.

Of course those close to the family knew that Glenn developed Alzheimer's and I guess he knew the progression of that horrible disease and kind of quit talking.

Keith said Alzheimer's took everything from Glen but it couldn't take his soul... powerful words.

Funerals

I hear Christians say frequently that "we just need to get to know each other better". One of the best ways to get to know people is to go to the funerals of their families.

This was an easy funeral for me to go to for a lot of reasons. The truth is that if they had charged admission I would have been happy to pay it.

Rest in eternity Glen Torno—you did well.

UNCLE ROB'S BLOG

Ofeilia Guzman Funeral

I went to the funeral for Ofelia Guzman today. I find that in this point of my life I'm attending more and more funerals. Today I got there early so I could have a seat and was visiting with all the people, learning family connections and giving my condolences. Luis Torres (Ofelia's brother-in-law) was the speaker and one thing he said that sticks in my mind was that he thought God had looked down on Ofelia and said "you've suffered enough...it's time to come home."

The Guzman's children attended at Parkway and I know them very well. Every time I see Ron he calls me "Quero" and every time I see him I call him "Uncle Ronnie" (because that's what his niece and nephew call him).

As we were filing out of the auditorium today and everyone was expressing condolences to the family I saw Uncle Ronnie sitting next to his Dad and the emotions hit me and all I could do was shake hands. See...you would think I would be prepared for that because it happens at every funeral I go to...but no it always catches me by surprise.

When I was standing by the hearse I was still choked up. Uncle Ronnie came up and said..."It's OK, Quero." But at the internment Uncle Ronnie was going around asking people if they needed anything (like water) and I said, "Yeah I'll take a Whataburger with cheese, fries and a coke and he grinned and said that's my Quero!"

I see my parent's generation quickly fading away and know that there are some big funerals awaiting me. We've lost three old timers at church this year and there are several more right behind them.

It's at times like these that we need God the most...when we hand over our most beloved to him to care for them forever.

I lost my Dad when he was 62 years old. I still ask God to find him and tell him that I love him.

Oh and by the way, Ron and Sylvia Guzman drove all the way from Corpus Christi to Houston to attend my Dad's funeral in 1998. I'll never forget that.

Funerals

I'm always torn about what would be best...for me to attend Julie's funeral or for her to attend mine. We're hoping that God takes us at the same time. We know there's no marriage in heaven but Julie says maybe we can hold hands.

I attend a lot of funerals and I'm glad to attend them because it reminds me that this life won't last forever and every day I live brings me one day closer to eternity.

Rest in eternal peace, Ofeilia...you have lived well.

Linda Magana Funeral

I had the opportunity this morning to attend the funeral of Linda Magana at Kostoryz Road Church of Christ. Linda was 58 years old…same as me. I didn't know her very well but know her parents, Salvador & Ruth Magana, quite well. Of course Ruth and her daughter Doris were members at Parkway many years ago.

I love the Hispanic culture. I love the South Texas ranching culture, the Mariachi bands, the food, the people and the pride that they take in their heritage. I like listening to Tex-Mex as it flows from Spanish to English in the same conversation. There was standing room only at the funeral today. I got to see a lot of old friends some of whom have been members at Parkway like Tony & Sulema Vasquez and Adolfo & Yole Lerma and Raul & Gina Torres. I got to see some of our friends from Cheyenne Street Church of Christ like Luis & Sylvia Torres and Jesse & Ophelia Guzman…and many others. I got to see Eddie "Poncho" Rodriguez who preaches at Norton Street Church of Christ.

I also like that at Parkway we have Anglo, Hispanic, Black and Asian people. For me it illustrates what God's Word does…it makes it so that people don't look at the outside physical characteristics but inwardly at the hearts of people. That's how God looks at people and that's how God's children look at each other. It's a wonderful testimony to Christ's deity…the miracle of changed lives.

I'm glad I got to go. God bless the Lord's church and God bless the Magana family.

Evangelism

UNCLE ROB'S BLOG

A Few Thoughts On Sharing God's Word With Other People

- It is God's Word that converts people to Christ. It's not me or you…it is God.

- What you teach depends on who you are teaching. Are you teaching an atheist? Then you need to teach about the existence of God. Are you teaching a Christian who is following a false system of belief? Then teach New Testament doctrines. Are you teaching someone who is morally bankrupt? Focus on what the Bible teaches about how we should live and what Jesus does for us.

- What is my objective as a teacher? It is not to vanquish or overwhelm someone with biblical superiority. It is not to get them to switch churches. My objective as a teacher should be to teach God's Word and build faith in God.

- As a teacher I should live a righteous, unselfish life. I should have a comprehensive knowledge of the scriptures. I must be intellectually honest and not be dogmatic and opinionated about questionable things. I must come to understand and know my student and I must be a learner. I must strive to be effective.

- Who can I teach? Those who are looking for spiritual help. Those who have an obvious need for spiritual help but are not looking for it.

- As a planter of God's Word I am not responsible for the outcome…God is. But still I can learn to be an effective, opportunistic teacher.

- The age of working miracles to get people's attention is over. We live in an age where the only miracle people will witness is the miracle of a godly life in an increasingly morally bankrupt society. That miracle is an attention getter and will create opportunities to teach.

Incredible Acts Of Heroism

I've been watching re-enactments on Netflix of the heroics of "Medal of Honor" winners. They are very emotional and very inspiring. One of the commentators said this,

"Once you cross the line that you are not going to survive anyway, then you are enabled to achieve incredible acts of heroism."

I've heard that sentiment before. They quit fighting for themselves and were just fighting to help their fellow soldiers survive. True sacrificial living on behalf of others.

Christian soldiers have a completely different mindset…I cannot be killed therefore I'm totally unafraid of what might happen to me (on earth) and am therefore completely free to testify about the Lord Jesus Christ to anyone who will listen.

In fact, that was exactly the mindset of the early Christian martyrs. Today you hear of Christians going into places like North Korea, Iran, China, etc. and you wonder…have they lost their minds? No they haven't, the bravest soldiers go where they are needed the most and understand that their "Medal of Honor" awaits them in heaven.

UNCLE ROB'S BLOG

"It's Easier To Believe The Bad Things"

The movie "Pretty Woman" tells the story of a young woman who made some poor choices, went down the wrong road and became a prostitute. One of her customers sees some good qualities in her and tries to get her to see those qualities. She has a hard time believing him and says something that has stuck in my brain for a long time. She says, "It's easier to believe the bad things."

Every level of self-doubt and lack of self-worth exists among people; I'm unlikeable because I'm not pretty, because I'm too heavy, because I'm handicapped, because I'm a failure, because I'm not good at anything, etc., etc., etc.

Self-doubt is crippling.

Jesus Christ had the ability to engage with the broken people of society and lift them up. He also empowered his people with the same ability.

People tend to respond positively if they feel that someone truly cares about them and won't give up on them no matter what.

Encouragement, edification and admonishment are powerful weapons when wielded by someone who truly cares and has demonstrated that care. Otherwise they are just empty words that fall on deaf ears.

Here's the challenge for the Christian warrior…find the most unlikeable person you can find and make them your true friend. Seek their company. Invite them into your home. Make them part of your lives. Be resilient and patient. Don't give up. The love of God which surpasses all understanding can cause a wonderful transformation to take place in them and in you.

Evangelism

Becoming Jesus

Second Corinthians 3:1–18 is a text that recalls when Moses was on Mount Sinai in the presence of God. That nearness had the effect of causing Moses' face to shine like the sun. In fact when Moses came down off the mountain he had to wear a veil over his face it was so bright. That is compared to what happens is in the presence of Jesus Christ. It is like looking into a spiritual mirror and viewing Jesus Christ. As we gaze into that mirror we are transformed into the same spiritual image.

There are at least three things involved in that transformation.

First John 5:18 states that those begotten of God do not sin; Jesus had no sin in him and we cannot have sin in us. We have to develop such a hatred for sin that it becomes impossible for us to engage in it.

Matthew 11:29 states that we are to take the "yoke" of Jesus and "learn" about him. If we're going to be transformed into the image of Jesus Christ we need to have a deep and intimate knowledge of who he is.

Philippians 2:1–7 states that Jesus was a servant and we must also become servants to each other…a community of servants. We can be transformed into the image of Jesus Christ by committing ourselves to being free of sin, by learning of Jesus and by living lives of service to others. We are not called upon to evangelize the world. We are called upon to become Jesus Christ. Take care of that and the world will be evangelized.

Helping The Lost

Romans chapter twelve describes the kind of life that God wants his people to live. These verses provide a model for Christian living that describes how God's people should interact with other people.

The purpose for this model is two fold. First, God's diagram for living provides for happy lives. God loves his people, he wants them to be happy and he wants his people to love him for what he does for them.

Secondly, this model for Christian living presents his greatest tool for bringing non-believers to him…his instructions personified in living form. The theory of Christian living becomes living and breathing fact.

1 Peter 3:15 says that non-believers will ask questions about God based on what they see in the lives of his followers. Christians are living conversion machines who don't necessarily have to go out seeking converts but who, because of the way they live, attract the converts to them.

So why don't we see more non-believers flocking into churches asking questions?

Because Christians tend to park their lives in churches and among friends who are already Christians or friends who aren't Christians but who lead pretty good lives. Or they just isolate themselves from everyone.

Jesus did his best work among the morally degraded people of his day…people who had wrecked their lives through the ravages of sinful excess.

My advice would be to share your lives with the kind of people Jesus shared his life with. We are after all powerfully equipped to turn these people to God and all we have to do is present our lives to those who need it the worst. The questions will come.

Edification for the Purpose of Evangelism

Edification is the process of building up people morally and spiritually. Evangelism is the sharing of knowledge for the purpose of conversion. Edification and evangelism are blood brothers to each other.

There are two ways people are brought to Christ; through individual action and through collective action. These two general actions are not mutually exclusive of each other and there is some sharing between the two.

The area of individual action is illustrated in 1 Peter 3. An individual leads such a morally exemplary life (via edification) that people ask questions about the cause for it. The individual then shares (via evangelism) the information with the questioner.

The area of collective action is illustrated in John 17:22–23. The world comes to believe in Jesus Christ through the "oneness" of the believers with each other and with God. The gospel has great power to change lives and to assemble from the rich/poor, black/white, young/old, tattooed/non-tattooed a group of people who forsake their differences for Jesus Christ.

These individuals are built spiritually (edification) into a collective (the church) for the purpose of sharing belief (evangelism) in Jesus Christ. The church and the individual are God's chosen tools to reach a lost world.

Do not neglect your responsibilities to grow spiritually as an individual and to grow spiritually as a church. If we fail in that, we've failed…the world.

Arm Wrestling And Benevolence

I did a little benevolence work tonight. Julie and I were in the Luby's parking lot after services tonight fixing to go in and get something to eat and a big black guy came up to me a little down on his luck and needing some work and some money. He had to be about 6'3" and pretty stout so I told him if he could beat me arm wrestling I would give him $10. He laughed and I don't think he thought I was serious but I slapped my arm down on the hood of the car and we arm wrestled. Even though I beat him I still gave him the $10.

But then he told me he needed work and he didn't have the best of records. I gave him my name and phone number and got his name and phone number and I think I may have a job lined up for him. We'll see. I do feel a special kinship with him though…arm wrestling does that for you.

If you need a worker…call me.

Leadership

Nehemiah: Prayer, Planning and Preparation

Nehemiah wanted to rebuild the wall surrounding Jerusalem. Here are the problems he faced and overcame.

- He didn't have the resources or the political backing he needed.

- He had non-Jewish enemies who were powerful and ridiculed him and plotted against him.

- He relied upon a volunteer labor force that was discouraged and poor and oppressed.

- He had Jewish enemies who fed information to his non-Jewish enemies and who conspired with them to bring him down.

Nehemiah was able to get the walls rebuilt in 52 days in spite of the great odds against him. He didn't just pray about it but also planned and prepared. Let's use that same formula to convert the world.

More Leadership From Nehemiah (Nehemiah 2:12-13)

And I arose in the night, I and a few men with me, I did not tell any one what my God was putting into my mind to do for Jerusalem and there was no animal with me except the animal on which I was riding.

So I went out by night...inspecting the walls of Jerusalem which were broken down and its gates which were consumed with fire."

Nehemiah took on the job of rebuilding the walls surrounding Jerusalem based on some intel he had received when he was in King Artaxerxes court. Shortly after he arrives in Jerusalem he makes a personal inspection of the wall at night...in secrecy. Nehemiah, as a great leader, recognizes that you can't just rely on reports...you have to have on-the-ground information.

Too often leaders are inundated with information which is out of context, overstated, understated or just completely wrong. It is imperative that leaders carefully assess the problem and make sure to hear all the sides of the story before acting. Other wise we can make decisions based on faulty information that cause more harm than good.

In addition, Nehemiah gathered his intel in secrecy. Nehemiah had enemies...enemies from the outside and enemies from the inside. Sometimes it's best not to reveal a plan of action until you have all your ducks lined up. Think about the number of times an idea has died in infancy because someone said..."that's a stupid idea" or "that will never work." Focus your energies in the planning and let the idea mature before you trot it out for public inspection. Leaders formulate solid plans based on solid information and then deal with obstacles as they arise.

Wow, How, and Wow/How

Nehemiah is a keen example of leadership. He identified a project (rebuilding the wall around Jerusalem) and built a team of people to complete that project. Let's consider a few things about Nehemiah.

- Nehemiah cared about the condition of Jerusalem without walls. He bought into it emotionally. Even though he had zero abilities at wall building he knew that with the help of God he could do it.

- Nehemiah fasted and prayed to God about the project. I don't know if God responded to him or if he did what God told him to do. People of faith, like Nehemiah, always go to God first.

- Nehemiah was the cup bearer for the king of the Medo-Persian empire. Nehemiah knew he would need the king's help and knew what kind of man the king was. So Nehemiah prepared for the one and only moment that would present itself.

- When the moment came Nehemiah presented the king with the scope and magnitude of the project, a time line, a materials list and a request for letters of authorization for safe passage.

- When Nehemiah arrived in Jerusalem he didn't know who his friends or who his enemies were so some level of secrecy was required and he went out at night by himself to view the project.

- Nehemiah assembled the people and communicated to them the need to rebuild the walls and a team was built on that day and the repair started.

- Nehemiah strengthened his team by writing down and naming who all was doing the work. He didn't take credit himself but gave all the credit to the workers. People like being identified.

- Enemies to the project arose. Those enemies included outsiders but also many insiders including some of the priests whose

Leadership

families had inter-married with the outsiders.. Again Nehemiah went directly to God in prayer for help with the enemies.

- ◆ Nehemiah had spies who learned of the enemies actions and Nehemiah was able to counter their evil plans.

- ◆ Nehemiah had the right to eat the delicate food that the king provided him but he refused to do so. He wanted to identify with the working people not the privileged royalty.

- ◆ Nehemiah identified for the people why the walls had been torn down in the first place and that the same behaviors still existed. Why rebuild a wall that is just going to be torn down again if the people aren't living righteously? So Nehemiah had the priests communicating God's word to the people.

Nowadays two types of people are commonly identified: "wow" people and "how" people. Wow people have lots of ideas and are volunteering them to anyone who will listen. "How" people listen to the ideas and say…"OK, have you given any thought to how your wow idea can be accomplished?"

So which one was Nehemiah? He was both…he was a "Wow-How" guy. Those types of people are pretty rare…except with God's help.

Have a "wow-type" of idea? Buy into it, ask for God's help (every day) and prepare, prepare, prepare and God will help you with the "How" and maybe…like Nehemiah…you can build a wall around God's city.

Personal Growth

The Rich Man and Lazarus
(Luke 16:19–31)

Lazarus was a beggar. I don't know how he came to be that way…maybe the same way people become beggars today; poor economic times, destructive life styles, mental illness, who knows? Lazarus was alone in the world with no one to help him. He was incapacitated and had skin sores and was hungry. Only the local dogs had compassion upon him…they licked his wounds. There are two Lazarus' mentioned in the New Testament. The other one had two sisters and when he died there was much sorrow and many tears. When the beggar Lazarus died he went to his grave unloved, unwept, and not missed.

The rich man on the other hand liked to dress nice and lived in "mirth and splendor" every day. He had a lot of friends and five brothers who loved him. I'm sure at his funeral there were many tears shed and accolades spoken…and yet the rich man ended up in "Hades."

You see, the rich man had a low opinion of beggars and after a while beggars just become a part of the landscape…like a fire hydrant. He probably thought Lazarus had "earned" his condition (like that makes a difference) and he wasn't going to support Lazarus in his poor choices. That thinking kind of makes sense but that thought process landed the rich man squarely in the fires of Hell.

I'm sure when Lazarus was born he was a beautiful little boy and his mom and dad were overjoyed to have him but somewhere along the way Lazarus lost the ability to work, lost his family, lost his health and lost the capacity to be liked. In the Hebrew language names mean things and Lazarus' name meant something…it meant "God has helped." I'm reminded of Jesus' words…blessed are the poor who are in a relationship with the Spirit for theirs is the Kingdom of Heaven. God does help.

Someone told me they kept a supply of Whataburger gift certificates in their wallet in case they came across someone who looked hungry…not a bad idea.

Criticism And Critics

At the gym where I work out there's a guy who does a handstand and then proceeds to do push-ups from the handstand. I was surprised to hear someone else say, "he's showing off."

It made me think that if you are living your life at a really high level or at a really low level then you are setting yourself up for criticism but if you are living your life at an average level you'll be OK. Everyone wants to be average.

Christians are supposed to be living their lives at really high levels in service to God, to each other and to the world. They are supposed to let their "lights shine brightly" so that people will be drawn to the light of Christ living in us.

Unfortunately some will even criticize that. We have to be careful about being critical people. Criticism, done the wrong way, can be emasculating.

I never thought that guy at the gym was showing off…it never entered my mind. Rather, it inspired me to be in better shape physically. We can choose to be inspired or we can choose to become critics.

Inspiration builds us up…being critical tears us and others down. Choose which you want to be. Heaven will only be filled with those who let their lights shine and who help others to be illuminating.

Anniversary Parties

We had a 10 year anniversary party at Tejas Veterinary Clinic last month. We invited all our clients to attend. It was very successful. What amazed me, and I guess it shouldn't have, was how motivated we were to clean the place up and spruce it up a little bit.

In fact, a lot of things I have just let slide over the years, all of a sudden I fixed up. That's human nature I suppose…if there's no deadline…we're not greatly motivated to do things.

It made me think of our lives and our accountability to God. It sure would be nice if God would just tell us when he's coming to judge the world. That way we could all be ready. I can just see it…all of a sudden people would start dealing with sin in their lives. Even some of the "gray" areas of sin would suddenly become "black and white" for us.

After all we would not want to take any chance that we could end up in Hell and suffer eternal condemnation. Who would risk that? Not only that but all of a sudden we would be looking for opportunities to serve others.

But you know what? I'm afraid that if God did actually give the exact date when he was coming back that there would be some "smart" guy who would wait right up to the day before judgment to make things right. Sort of sneak in right at the last minute. And that's not what God wants in people.

He doesn't want folks who are trying to beat the system. He wants people who believe in him and are so grateful that they want to be exactly the kind of people God wants them to be. I guess it's better for God not to announce the exact day when he's coming. We need to adjust ourselves to God's plan and not try to adjust God's plan to ourselves.

Spiritual Triage

A while back the Parkway men used to have a breakfast once a month at a local eatery. Breakfast isn't really my thing and for me usually a cup of coffee suffices. I came in late for one of the breakfasts and of course the guys gave me a hard time about being late and that's OK...I expect it because I distribute a lot of grief myself.

Anyway, they were on me for being late and I told them that on the way in I saw a young woman with three kids broke down on the side of the road and stopped to help her. I prayed for them and wished them well and went merrily on my way. Of course that story was completely fictitious but it did shut them up (briefly).

Of course James 2:14 states, "What good is it brethren if a man claims to have faith but has no deeds. Can such a faith save him?"

The scripture talks in multiple places about the importance of prayer and how we should be praying continually. But there is a time for prayer and a time for action. Don't be so involved in spiritual activities like prayer, Bible study, singing, etc. that you fail to act when action is required.

Of course if I had actually seen the young woman with three small children stranded on the side of the road the appropriate action would have been to stop and address her actual need...we could always have prayed afterwards.

UNCLE ROB'S BLOG

Humility Contests

Some of you know that several years ago Julie made a comment that one of our members was "the humblest man she had ever met." Of course I said "what…more humble than me?" And I told her, "I could be the humblest guy at church and start a humility contest with the other guys.

In retrospect, maybe that humility contest thing is not such a bad idea and what would that look like anyway? A lot of people have the wrong idea about what humility is and think that humility is incongruous with a strong personality or a lot of confidence in ones abilities. So before we can see what a humility contest looks like we first have to understand the Bible definition of humility.

> Have this mind among yourselves, which is yours in Christ Jesus, who, though he was in the form of God, did not count equality with God a thing to be grasped, but made himself nothing, taking the form of a servant, being born in the likeness of men. And being found in human form, he humbled himself by becoming obedient to the point of death, even death on a cross. Therefore God has highly exalted him and bestowed on him the name that is above every name (Philippians 2:5–11).

Jesus Christ our supreme example in everything was also supreme in the attribute of humility. He had a strong personality, strong self-confidence and was very forthright in his speech and yet…humble.

Jesus Christ was humble because he served others. He gave up his rights and his life to serve humanity.

So get this…humility has nothing to do with a quiet nature/personality but has everything to do with helping and serving others. So what would a humility contest look like? It would look like people sacrificing their time, energy and resources to help other people out.

That original humility contest thing was a big joke because the motivation was misplaced. Our real motivation to be humble is to serve God and defeat Satan. We do that by killing the self-serving pride in our lives and by cultivating and nurturing selfless humility.

Personal Growth

What To Do About Anger

The book of Proverbs gives a lot of advice on how to live better lives. One of the recurring themes is being "slow to anger." Anger leads to impulsive actions and a chain of events that can have permanent detrimental consequences. Consider the next five passages.

> Whoever is slow to anger is better than the mighty, and he who rules his spirit than he who takes a city (Proverbs 16:32).

> The beginning of strife is like letting out water, so quit before the quarrel breaks out (Proverbs 17:14).

> A hot tempered man stirs up strife, but he who is slow to anger quiets contention (Proverbs 15:18).

> A soft answer turns away wrath, but a harsh word stirs up anger (Proverbs 15:1).

> The heart of the wise makes his speech judicious and adds persuasiveness to his lips (Proverbs 16:23).

One of the biggest problems folks face today is anger and its consequences. Consequences include; unhappy homes, unhappy workplaces and breaking both the laws of man and of God. A person's anger can land him in jail and in hell.

Sometimes we control our anger but it spills out on others. Have you ever found yourself to have internal anger that causes you to be an unpleasant person and spills out upon the innocent? Just controlling anger for the moment is not the answer.

The good news is that not only can we can train ourselves to control our anger, but we can also become the type of people who can defuse the anger of others. It's all in God's book…the Bible. What are we waiting on?

UNCLE ROB'S BLOG

Human Behaviors in Luke 9

Not long after Jesus was "transfigured" on the mountain the Gospel of Luke records three incidents in which Jesus had to correct the behavior of his disciples.

The first incident (Luke 9:46) the disciples were discussing who of the disciples were the greatest. Jesus took a little child and told them that the disciple who cares more about little children than about the noble of the world was the greatest disciple.

The second incident (Luke 9:49) occurred when John, the beloved disciple, saw a fellow casting out demons and told him not to do it because he was not one of the ones following Jesus. Jesus told John to leave the guy alone.

The third incident (Luke 9:54) occurred when James and John were insulted by the negligent actions of some Samaritan villagers and wanted to kill them suggesting to Jesus that he send down fire from the sky to do so. Jesus rebuked them for their anger towards the villagers.

Sometimes we are just like these disciples, we focus on personal achievement and fame when we should be focusing on the needs of others…especially the needs of those who can't help themselves.

Sometimes we're quick to condemn other religious groups who are doing wonderful things for Christ because they may not understand the Bible just like we do.

And sometimes we are too easily offended and tend to over react against those who have offended us.

Jesus knew the weaknesses in his disciples and worked with them until they overcame those weaknesses. He's patient and working with us too.

Satan And Peter

In Luke 22:31, Jesus informed Peter that Satan had asked permission to tempt Peter and Jesus had granted permission. I wonder why Satan chose Peter? I think I know why.

Satan knows all the followers of Jesus including you and I. Satan picked out Peter because he knew Peter was dangerous and important to Jesus.

Satan knew that Peter was the one in Matthew 16 who identified Jesus as the "Christ...the Son of the Living God."

Satan knew that because of that confession Jesus had granted Peter the honor of opening the doors to the Kingdom of Heaven by preaching the first Gospel message on the day of Pentecost.

Satan knew that Peter was one of three special disciples chosen by Jesus to witness his transfiguration.

Satan likes a challenge and always has. With God's permission he personally tempted Job, one of God's best people. He tempted Jesus in the wilderness and finally he tempted one of Jesus' best soldiers...Peter.

Satan singles out God's best for temptation because the routine temptations of earthly living aren't enough to cause God's best to fail. Prepare yourselves to give your best to God and prepare yourselves to receive Satan's worst and in so doing prepare yourselves for eternal blessings from God.

UNCLE ROB'S BLOG

Why 40 Days In the Wilderness?

The first thing Jesus did after he was baptized and had received the Holy Spirit was to go to the wilderness to allow Satan to tempt him. We get some details about that temptation.

Satan thought he had found a weak point and was going to put his finger on it and suggested to Jesus since he hadn't had a thing to eat for 40 days that Jesus should turn a stone into a loaf of bread and eat it.

The thing I want you to notice about this is that Jesus had the power to turn a rock into bread and he could have done so and enjoyed a meal with Satan but Jesus, unlike a lot of humanity, wanted nothing to do with Satan.

So Satan decides next to tempt Jesus with power and showed Jesus all the kingdoms of the world and offered Jesus authority over all of them if he would only do one small thing…bow down before Satan and worship him. A lot of humanity wouldn't give that a second thought. They would drop right to their knees and revere Satan for the power to control all the countries of the world and think that they had pulled one over on old Satan.

Jesus wouldn't do it because it was wrong to give something to Satan that only belonged to God and nothing Satan could offer was worth offending God. We're quick to engage in things that are wrong because we know God loves us and is forgiving. Be careful you might get tangled up in that rope. You belong to God. Don't give what is God's to Satan.

The last desperate attempt of Satan was to take a stab at Jesus' pride. Satan led with a scripture this time. He quoted Psalm 91 in which the promise is made that God would send angels to protect his righteous one from harm.

With this scripture Satan invited Jesus to Jump off the highest point of the temple to see if God would send angels to protect him. Jesus answered with Deuteronomy 6:16, "Thou shall not make trial of the Lord your God." You don't have to accept every challenge that is thrown at you. You can walk away.

Why did Jesus start his ministry by allowing Satan to tempt him?

Personal Growth

Because he knew that when believers began their ministry after being baptized that Satan would attack them too. And to show them that it is possible to be tempted by Satan and to conquer him. Gather yourself up and get about your spiritual business and don't worry and moan about Satan. He is a coward and you can beat him…just like Jesus did.

Slaves And Slave Owners

The letter to Philemon is about a runaway slave named Onesimus who was owned by Philemon and somehow made it to Rome where the Apostle Paul was imprisoned by the Roman government awaiting trial.

Somewhere along the way Onesimus hears about Jesus Christ and becomes a Christian and a friend and helper of Paul.

This makes me wonder a few things...Paul could have asked/demanded that Philemon free the slave Onesimus or he could have offered to purchase Onesimus or he could have asked Philemon to loan Onesimus to him. Instead he sends Onesimus back to Philemon.

My guess is that if he had done any of these things (besides sending Onesimus back) that Philemon could have felt that he was being taken advantage of. After all Philemon could have had a significant investment in Onesimus especially if Onesimus had a particularly valuable skill set. It might have been, as Paul alluded to, that the slave Onesimus might have stolen from Philemon. All these things have to be considered as possibilities.

So Paul was very careful about how he handled this situation...after all it could have turned out to have a negative impact on the kingdom. Paul's handling of this situation demonstrated skill and concern about all parties involved. By sending Onesimus back, Paul demonstrated both Philemon's legal right to Onesimus and Onesimus' legal obligation to Philemon. So Paul was acting in a way that dealt honorably with the Law.

It was almost a certainty that Philemon would act honorably towards Onesimus and perhaps even free him. Paul in his writing to Philemon in an understated way reminded Philemon of his obligations to Paul. Presumably Paul converted Philemon to Jesus Christ and perhaps as an apostle laid hands upon him and imparted some spiritual gift. Philemon was under a tremendous spiritual debt to Paul.

The bottom line is that Paul demonstrated great skill and consideration so that the Kingdom could be elevated and not diminished. What a great lesson...can we do any less?

Stormy Seas And Faith

Mark 4 records in just one paragraph a story of Jesus and his disciples in a boat when a storm whips up. The disciples wake Jesus exclaiming "Teacher do you not care that we are about to perish?" at which time Jesus spoke the winds and rough seas into silence.

Jesus didn't include this story in the Gospel narrative because he was short on miracles or needed to fill a little space.

Jesus had just taught on the shore of this very sea some stories about the coming Kingdom. He taught about sowing seed and the productivity of faith planted in a faithful heart. He also taught about the of how a seed is transformed into a plant and the coming harvest. Lastly he taught that the kingdom was like a planted mustard seed and how such a small seed could turn into a big plant.

And then at the culmination of this teaching about the Kingdom he gets into a boat and crosses the sea and the winds blow, the sea is churned up and the disciples fear that they are going to drown. Like they expected the headlines of the Jerusalem newspaper the next morning would read…"Jesus and Disciples Drown During Freak Storm on the Sea of Galilee."

It's like they haven't been listening…nothing can stop the coming of the Kingdom and their role in it…not stormy seas, not earthquakes, nothing can stop the Kingdom!

Jesus included this story at the culmination of his teaching to test their understanding and their faith and they came up a little short in the faith department. But…that's okay because the building of faith is a process and Jesus was patient with his disciples just as God is patient with us.

There may be some stormy seas ahead of us too but just remember…Jesus can calm the stormiest of seas. Have a little faith in him because he has a plan for us.

Thirty Pieces Of Silver

I was reading Matthew 26–27 the other day and thinking about Judas' betrayal of Jesus for 30 pieces of silver. I suspect that Judas may not have known that this betrayal would lead to Jesus' death. After all, Judas had witnessed Jesus' great power and miracle working. He may have suspected that Jesus would triumph over anything the chief priests could bring against him. I don't know.

What I do know is that when Judas witnessed the events that would lead to Jesus' death he became very remorseful. So remorseful that he tried to correct his sin by confessing it to the chief priests and elders. Precisely what he should have done under Old Testament Law. He even offered restitution by giving the money back. Instead of forgiving Judas the chief priests rejected his repentance. They had to. If they had accepted his repentance it would be an admission of their own guilt. They couldn't do that. They couldn't offer Judas forgiveness and let him walk away.

Judas was so remorseful that he went out and hanged himself. Imagine the level of remorse that would cause someone to place a noose around their neck and cause themselves to be strangled to death. Judas had remorse. Sometimes we wonder why he didn't go to Jesus and ask for forgiveness? I think the answer has to be that Judas did not fully believe in Jesus. Oh, he believed in Jesus' power and miracle working but he did not believe that Jesus could or would forgive him of this great sin.

It's always about belief isn't it? Jesus could have forgiven Judas but Judas had no faith in him. Faith can solve all our problems.

Personal Growth

What Must I Do To Inherit Eternal Life?

In Matthew 19:16–22, a man asks Jesus a question, "What must I do to inherit eternal life?" That's a great question…almost like a practice test before the judgment day.

Imagine if Jesus could do a brief review of our spiritual condition and tell us what we have to work on. What a blessing! We potentially could be much better prepared to face the judgment. Jesus' first answer to the man was to tell him to follow the 10 Commandments as they relate to how we treat other people; don't murder anyone, don't cheat on your wife, don't steal, don't lie, don't cheat and give honor to your parents. Check. Check. Check. Check. Check. Check. Then Jesus told the man something that is never mentioned in the 10 Commandments. Sell everything you have and become a disciple and follow Jesus. The man had to think on that one and walked away with sorrow because he highly valued his possessions. Six out of seven things he was OK on. In school that would be an 86…definitely passing and above average but in the kingdom not good enough to go to heaven.

Christians have to put greater value on compassion for the poor than for their personal financial well-being. Jesus after all gave up everything he had to help those in spiritual poverty and we are to be like him. If not then say adios to eternal life. The only test we're going to get before the judgment day is a self-test and it's an open book test. Don't neglect to make use of it.

Making Grapes

Prior to his crucifixion Jesus had a long conversation with his disciples. He was preparing them for when he would be gone and for what their duties would be after he was gone.

In, John 15:1–8, he told them that he had some expectations of them…they would need to be productive. He explained this by comparing them to grape vines. In the vineyard the master gardener evaluated the productivity of different branches of the grape plant. If a branch was not productive it would be removed. If a branch was producing a lot of grapes it could be pruned so that it would produce even more grapes. God is the gardener. Jesus is the plant. We are the branches.

One can be a grape branch that is producing a lot of leaves, is robust and is pleasing to the eye. One can also be a grape branch that may not have many leaves but is loaded up with grapes.

God is not interested in people who just look like good Christians. Our works of service to others is the most beautiful thing to him. Let's make some grapes.

Hospitality

Friendliness vs. Hospitality

Parkway is a pretty friendly congregation but friendliness is a subset of hospitality and is not equal to hospitality. Hospitality is bigger than friendliness.

We've been talking in our elder qualification class about hospitality and understand that although hospitality is an imperative for elders it is required of all Christians. Here are some suggestions for being hospitable to new members.

- ◆ Share a meal with the new members. Either at home or in a restaurant.

- ◆ If you can't share a meal make some cookies or give a small gift along with saying something like…"welcome to the congregation."

- ◆ Since new members are new to town recommend auto repair shops, doctors, dentists, restaurants, etc.

- ◆ Give your cell number to them along with saying something like…"If you're ever in a bind or just want to talk…call me."

- ◆ Find them on Facebook and send a "friend" request.

My goal is that every single member of the congregation would act hospitably to our new members.

Customer Service

Julie and I were in New Orleans a few weeks ago and were scheduled to go to a lunch put on by a drug company. We were a little early and Julie was hungry so we walked into the hotel restaurant where they were still serving a breakfast buffet. I asked how much it was and the server said $28. Julie said…I'll just wait and walked out.

The server said…if she wants a muffin I'm sure that will be okay. So I fetched my bride and she picked out a blueberry muffin. As we were walking out the server ran to us and said…here's a napkin.

Wow! That's customer service.

How about "customer service" in our assemblies…specifically our visitors? Do we ignore them or give them a warm welcome and act as if we are truly interested in them. Do we judge them because they may be dressed inappropriately or do we ignore their dress for the sake of being hospitable? Are body piercings and tattoos so repulsive to us that it creates a barrier to hospitality?

I was paid a compliment by a former employer who is not known for paying compliments. He said, "Rob Perkins can talk to anyone, no matter their station in life, and make them feel comfortable." That compliment really goes to my mother because I learned hospitality from her. Learn hospitality. Don't be too busy and neglect visitors and don't judge based on appearance. Practice excellent "customer service."

That server at the Ritz Carlton in New Orleans? I told her if she wanted a job I would gladly hire her. She is a precious jewel. I hope that visitors at Parkway can see the same qualities in us.

Visitors ... Make The Most Of An Opportunity

Visitors to congregations are very important...especially local visitors. Local visitors are usually visiting either because they feel some acute need for a connection with God or they are looking for a place to become a member.

I love interacting with visitors. I try to put myself in their position and ask myself what I would want to see when visiting a congregation.

The first thing I would want to see is if anyone cared that I was there (besides the preacher). Like...how many people introduced themselves to me or...was it just a superficial greeting like..."Howdy glad to have you come back again."

Someone who is artful in the mechanics of conversation will use the Socratic method of asking questions and letting them do most of the talking like...1) Where are you from? 2) Oh you're from in town? How did you hear about us? 3) Where have you been attending?

You also want to make a personal connection and ask a question like...what kind of work do you do? Oh! You're a welder...so am I or if you are not a welder then you can introduce them to someone else who is a welder or whatever occupation they are.

The second thing I want them to see in our congregation is racial diversity. Especially in our day and age of charges of racism I want the visitor to see people of every color in our congregation.

Thirdly I want them to see that our hour of worship is inspiring. People are singing their hearts out. I don't want them to hear a "canned" prayer but one that is heartfelt and inspiring and perhaps relates to things that are troubling about our society today...a contemporary prayer. I want them to hear a sermon that makes them want to come back and hear another.

Generally you only have one shot at a visitor so I want to try to make it as memorable as I can.

For the two individual visitors today I asked them each individually if I could buy their lunches today. They both turned me down but that invitation should be burned into their memories. I don't think I have ever visited a church where a member has invited me to dinner.

Usually I write my name and number down and give it to them and let them know I have lived here a long time and know the best mechanics, plumbers, AC people, etc. in town. Several have taken advantage of that offer.

I also try to find them on Facebook and send a friend request. In addition, I take a photo of their visitor card and share it on our private Parkway member page to give the rest of our team (who are on FB) an opportunity to get involved.

Visitors are very important. We might be able to help them with some spiritual need or we might be able to add them to our local army of Christian soldiers in our fight against Satan.

Take the opportunity to be hospitable because you may not get another chance and maybe...God sent that person to test and reward you.

Perfect Hospitality

Then Jesus said to his host, "When you give a luncheon or dinner, do not invite your friends, your brothers or sisters, your relatives, or your rich neighbors; if you do, they may invite you back and so you will be repaid. But when you give a banquet, invite the poor, the crippled, the lame, the blind, and you will be blessed. Although they cannot repay you, you will be repaid at the resurrection of the righteous" (Luke 14:12–14 NIV).

Hospitality is huge in building congregations and individual Christians. It is the theory of Christianity put into practice. After all, Jesus said that the world would recognize us by our love/hospitality for each other. Sometimes Christians can fool themselves into thinking they are hospitable when in fact they are self-serving by only being hospitable to those who are hospitable in kind.

That is a type of hospitality but not the "type" or level that is characteristic of a faithfully mature Christian. If you want to really please God be hospitable to widows, to the socially inept, to the mentally unsound, to the people that you have the least in common with and who the world has little care for. If you do that, God will hug you when you enter heaven and tearfully say "thank you for helping my people."

Three Cases of Hospitality

We find three test cases of hospitality in Genesis 18–19.

The first is when the Lord and two angels disguised as men visit Abraham. Abraham believing that they were mere men rushed from his tent, bowed down and offered to wash their feet. He had his servants slaughter a young calf to feed them and had his wife Sarah make fresh bread for them.

The second case was when the two angels, disguised as men, went to the city of Sodom. Lot was sitting at the gates when they approached. Like Abraham he approached the men and bowed down and offered to wash their feet and invited them into his home. At first the men (angels) said no we'll just sleep out in the city square but Lot insisted and they accepted his hospitality.

The third case of hospitality was when the men of Sodom found out there were men visiting their city. They surrounded Lot's home and wanted to greet the men by having gang rape homosexual sex with them.

Christians are supposed to be hospitable too. Will we be like Abraham and Lot who bowed down in humility and offered to feed and house our visiting guests? Will we be like Lot who didn't accept the declination of the visitors but insisted upon serving them? Or will we be like the men of Sodom who wanted to take advantage of these strangers? Or will we be somewhere in the middle ground…nice to meet you…hope you have a nice visit. Or will we just ignore the strangers and walk right past them?

God's people are supposed to be known for their hospitality…like Abraham and Lot. Their hospitality cost them something…time and money.

Elders

Eldership And Member Development

Obviously the congregation is made up of different members with differing abilities. The church is described in 1 Corinthians 12 as a human body. The body needs all of its parts to function properly. If parts are absent or weakened then the church is "handicapped" and cannot function properly as God designed it.

So then it is on the Elders to identify and develop talent in the congregation so that the church body can function properly.

Here's the thing…talent can never be developed unless it is discovered and used.

Several things factor into the wasting of talent by not using it. In a lot of congregations the preacher is the main guy. He typically does all the preaching and teaches all of the classes. After all that's his job we pay him for that, right?. So you have a body part that is over developed while the other parts are wasting away. I'm not a fan of the one preacher system (for several reasons) where the preacher is used to the exclusion of the other members.

Another factor is micromanagement by elders. Some elders feel like they have to do and control everything. I know of some congregations where the elders do all of the announcements for fear that someone might "announce" the wrong thing.

At Parkway we discovered a young man who in his early 20s had an incredible "presence" for making announcements. He was comfortable, spoke clearly and had good extemporaneous thoughts to share with the congregation. We have used him and I'm convinced still have not discovered his "ceiling."

We've had young Song-leaders who showed ability and with use have really developed into excellent song leaders.

Talent and ability can never grow unless you use them. You can't be afraid of talent making mistakes. In fact you want the talented people to make mistakes so they can grow and learn from it.

Elders

As elders, let's not handicap the congregation. Let's discover talent and use that talent so the congregation can be all that it can be.

How To Discover And Develop Talent

The parable of the pounds (Luke 19:11–27) has two stories going on in it. The one we're interested in has a master giving 1 pound each to 10 of his servants. The master is going on an extended trip and tells his servants to invest his money and when he gets back there will be an accounting to see how they did.

When he gets back we see only the results of three of the servants...the two most profitable ones and the guy who did the worst. The star of the class was the fellow who invested his pound and made 10 more pounds. The master was very happy with him and praised him and put him in charge of ten cities.

The second guy took his pound and made five more. The master put him in charge of five cities.

The last guy was governed by the fear of losing his investment principle and instead of investing it...hid it and preserved it for his master. The master was very unhappy with him and punished him by taking the pound away from him and giving it to his star performer.

How to Discover and Develop Talent.

1. People have to be given an opportunity to perform. In this story the master did not judge the abilities of his employees. He treated them all the same. They all started on the exact same footing and had the same opportunity.

2. When a responsibility is given to someone there has to be an accounting or evaluation process.

3. Finally, after the evaluation process those who have performed well need to be rewarded (positively reinforced) and those who have not performed well must be reprimanded (negatively reinforced).

The master gave opportunity to 10 of his employees and discovered a really high performing individual who he groomed to be even better. He also discovered an employee who was a disaster.

This may sound like advice on how to run a business but it is really about God's people and the church.

Drought

We've been in a drought here in South Texas since before January. We really never had a spring it's been so dry. Of course you can keep the plants alive with city water but they really don't thrive. To compound that in early February we had a historic freeze that killed a lot of vegetation that wildlife lives on. So it's been pretty sad around here.

For the past two days we've had rain…four inches of rain at my house. This morning when I got up and went outside the white wing dove were singing their hearts out and as I checked our plants they were putting on new growth and leafing out.

That city water has been worked over pretty hard by the water department and is laden with chemicals so it can be safe for our consumption. It can keep plant life alive but just barely. The water that falls out of the heavens is really what vegetation needs and thrives on…and it's what people need too.

I see congregations that are watered with "city water." The water has been sanitized, chemically treated, bottled up and labeled by human beings. When congregations are fed this kind of water they're kind of like plants…stunted and not much growth, collectively or individually.

When congregations are fed the "living" water which comes from heaven people are growing spiritually and the congregation is growing collectively because people would rather live in and are attracted to a garden watered from heaven.

As leaders let's do our best to provide what the plants in God's garden need…the kind of water they can thrive and grow on. And if we look at our "work" and see that it's stunted and sad let's take a long look at what we're doing and make whatever corrections we can.

Eldership and Wives

The qualification in I Timothy 3 states that an elder candidate "Must be the husband of one wife." Usually there is a reason behind qualifications and one reason is that the man must be a family man and demonstrate good leadership qualities in his own family so that the congregation can predict his ability to lead God's family. Not a bad reason but probably not the only reason.

Julie and I were married in 1973 one week out of high school. She remains some 43 years later the only girl I ever dated. When I became an elder at Parkway she fully supported me in that…of course. Over the course of time I have seen her excel as a Bible class teacher. To this day I can still say she is stronger in the Old Testament than I am. Gradually I saw her taking on other tasks. Tasks that I never asked or hinted that she do. As you know I send out via email my "Church News." She started copying that and handing it out to people who don't have email…primarily older people. Her weekly "Church News" is different than mine. Hers includes a prayer list, plus all the emails that I have sent out to the rest of the congregation during the week. In addition, she'll add anything encouraging that she might find.

Speaking of the "Prayer List" she is the one who maintains and updates that. I just forward it on.

She also keeps up the "Membership Roster" which includes email addresses, birthdays and anniversaries.

Every once in a while someone will thank me for an anniversary or birthday card. Everyone in the congregation receives those but they are not from me…they are from her signed "Rob and Julie Perkins." By the way, she doesn't get as many thanks as the number of cards she sends out but she has never complained about that.

She sees needs and encourages me to do something about it.

A while back I closed my fist and told her jokingly she was "quenching my spirit." She said, "I have been trying for 40 years to quench your spirit and so far have been unsuccessful." And yet a while back I had 3–4 members kind of down on me and said (for the first time), "sometimes it just doesn't seem worth it." A few days later she told me some things about what a fine elder she thought I was and some other kind things and a light came on and I said, "this is about what I said the other day?"

She is vital in organizing church pot lucks like the one we just had.

She's a quiet person and some people don't understand her. Several years ago one of our Hispanic members asked me if she was prejudiced. No she's just quiet and not as extroverted as I am. She doesn't like attention drawn to herself and I'm sure I'll be in trouble for this but I wanted to illustrate what an elder's wife can do working behind the scenes and not seeking the limelight and how she has helped transform me.

I'll never forget the day when a light clicked on for me and I thought, *She believes in me.*

The scriptures say he who finds a good wife finds a good thing…and in the case of this elder…the congregation finds a good thing as well.

Elder's Qualities

I've been studying the qualifications for elders recently and thought it might be a good exercise based upon those studies to write down a few qualities that I would like to see in an elder.

- ◆ Someone who is a skilled and effective Bible teacher who inspires me with their knowledge and wisdom.
- ◆ Someone who is not selfish but lives to help others.
- ◆ Someone who can listen to both sides of an issue.
- ◆ Someone who inspires me with their prayers.
- ◆ Someone who sacrifices everything for the benefit of the congregation.
- ◆ Someone who knows me and demonstrates personal concern and love for me.
- ◆ Someone who has a marriage that inspires me and whose children love and respect them.
- ◆ Someone who cares about the lost.
- ◆ Someone who I can laugh and cry with.
- ◆ Someone who I look up to and would like to be like.
- ◆ Someone who believes the best about everyone.

Eldership and Communicating Your Mission

I'm afraid that for many members if you asked them what the mission of the church was they would reply…to take the Lord's Supper, sing, give the offering, pray and listen to preaching…Failure…abject failure.

Those things are "what" the church does. The mission relates to "why" we do those things. We do the "what" things to accomplish the "why" things.

The Lord's Supper causes us to remember Jesus and his sacrifice. Singing is a memory device to teach us about God and to teach each other. The offering teaches us to sacrifice to help others. Praying teaches us dependence upon God for all of our cares and worries. Preaching/teaching causes us to learn about God. These things (and others) help us grow spiritually as individuals and collectively as a congregation to demonstrate to the world (physical world and spiritual world) that Jesus Christ is the Son of God.

That's our mission and it's a grand and challenging mission.

So elders, as leaders, need to constantly communicate to the congregation why we are in business. Not just a collection of spiritual robots performing a mundane list of requirements but a living, breathing, growing, organic collection of spiritual beings waging war with Satan and pleasing our God and Father in Heaven.

Eldership: Seating, Texting, etc.

Many years ago Julie and I used to sit towards the front of the auditorium and then for some reason we decided to change our seats and moved to the very back row. That turned out to be a good move for us. Here's what I've learned.

As an elder when you are sitting on the back row you can see the whole flock. When you are sitting in the front you can't. Things that can be seen from the back include things like who is missing, visitors and any activities that might need to be addressed.

Sometimes strangers with requests including homeless come in after services have started. It's good to have a person in authority in the back to address those folks.

Sometimes members come up to me with a note about something that needs to be announced when they ordinarily would not feel comfortable walking to the front to give said note.

Sometimes I see members crying during the services or who walk out crying that may have needs that I can address.

I do a little bit of texting during the services. If there is some kind of issue I can text the other elders and inform them. If there is a security issue where the security person in the back may need a little help I can text the other security people.

If there are several visitors who need to be greeted after services and I know I can't get to all of them I can text my other hospitality experts to help out.

Once services have started I can assess who is missing and text a message that we have missed them.

When the kids are filing out to go to class I can give them all a "fist bump."

One of the down sides to sitting on the back row is some of the members like to slap me on the back of the head or tap me on the opposite shoulder to make me look the wrong way. Just joking…that's not a downside…they're telling me that they love me.

Elders

I'm not saying that all the elders need to sit on the back row but at least one does because it's hard to shepherd the flock when you can't see the flock.

Julie and I didn't move to the back row because we did some in depth analysis or because of the wise council of a spiritual sage. We did it by accident and like a lot of things in our lives it just worked out for the good.

Eldership And How the Church Functions

You might see different things when you walk into a church service.

- ◆ Some churches are heavy on formality and ritualism and some are very casual and informal.

- ◆ Some churches emphasize the Bible and Bible study. Some who emphasize Bible study may put much more emphasis on the New Testament than the Old.

- ◆ Some churches are heavy on the social aspect of Christianity and the whole assembly may be punctuated with meals and snacks and such like with minimal Bible study.

- ◆ Some churches emphasize acceptance of other people to the extent that they ignore open sin and do not hold their members to any level of accountability.

- ◆ Some churches emphasize the positive aspects of God and de-emphasize God's hatred of sin.

All the examples listed above are examples of churches who are out of balance. The dangerous thing about out of balance churches is that they may produce Christians who are also out of balance.

The church functions to assist in the production of Christians who are the mirror images of Jesus Christ. To do so elders must lead the congregations they have authority over by teaching the Bible in a comprehensive way…a balance of the Old Testament and the New Testament. Elders must not neglect the powerful social aspect of the gospel of Christ and must encourage its members to fulfill their social obligations to each other. Elders should inform the congregation's members that Jesus wanted his people to be sin-free and that open sin in the congregation will not be ignored.

Elders should give careful consideration to how the congregations they work with function so that on the day when these congregations of people are delivered up to God for evaluation they may be found healthy and whole.

The Work Of Elders

As shepherds of a flock elders have responsibility for the care of individual Christians and the collectivity of Christians…the church.

Ephesians 4 clearly states that elders are to help individual Christians grow to full spiritual maturity…they are to resemble Jesus Christ. That is accomplished by helping individuals to fully understand God, by teaching them to eliminate sin in their lives and by encouraging them to put the needs of others before their own. The purpose of this process is to attract others to Jesus Christ by the power of a transformed life.

John 17 also clearly states that the unified relationship between Christians is the primary evidence to humanity of the deity of Jesus Christ. In fact, the church (the collectivity of Christians) not only testifies to humanity but also to the spirit world (Ephesians 3:10) the wisdom of God in sending his son to the world he created.

So elders work to help Christians not only get along well together but to build relationships that unify them in every sense of the word. They do this by removing members whose purpose seems to be to divide the flock (Acts 20), by addressing sin in members (1 Corinthians 5) that damages the image of the church, by mitigating problems between members and by encouraging members to express through deeds their love for each other.

God has given elders/shepherds a huge responsibility and in my opinion will hold them accountable for it.

Elder Qualifications Retrospectively

A study of qualifications (apostle, daily ministration, elder, deacon, widows indeed), reveal that the respective qualifications are applicable to the specific work being qualified for.

For instance the qualification for an apostle was that the individual had to have been in the company of Jesus from the time Jesus was baptized until the time he ascended into heaven. Undoubtedly he had to have other attributes as well but this was the distinctive one as related to the work of an apostle, i.e., he was to give personal testimony about Jesus Christ.

So then, when we consider elder qualifications they should be interpreted as how they impact the elder's "work." For instance most of the elder qualifications relate to his character. That's relevant to his work because according to Ephesians 4 he is to help Christians grow into the very image of Jesus Christ. He cannot do that unless he has first done it in his own personal life.

In addition, the man must be the husband of one wife. Why? Because the marital relationship mimics the relationship between Christians. In marriage the two become one flesh by mutual sacrifice and subjection. That's the same process in becoming "married" to Jesus Christ, individually and collectively (Ephesians 5). If the elder hasn't experienced that process in his own marriage then he is scarcely qualified to instruct others in the spiritual marriage process.

The man must have children and have successfully parented them. Fathers don't give up on their children. Like the father of the prodigal son, he may not tolerate bad behavior but he is always ready to forgive and restore. In a congregation of believers sometimes it is easier to just get rid of an unruly member but a "father" works to the best of his ability to correct an unruly son. Job prayed for his children and sacrificed for them just in case they might have sinned. Imagine what it would be like to have an elder in a congregation who expressed genuine care in the same manner.

Elders

Qualifications are germane to the work of an elder and should be studied in that light. First let's understand how God wants his elders to work within the church and then perhaps we can understand the qualifications better.

My Advice To Young Men Concerning Preparing Themselves To Be Elders

- Don't seek the office, let the office seek you.

- Work hard to be the best servant of God you can be. The rest of it (being an elder) will take care of itself.

- Dedicate yourselves to understanding the Bible. Know the Old Testament as well as you know the New Testament. A lot of problems in the church are a direct result of weak knowledge.

- Learn to be an effective teacher. Study those who are effective at teaching and imitate them.

- Search out opportunities to teach.

- Live what you teach. Don't be a hypocrite.

- Work on being a good husband and a good father. Those relationships are the training ground for leading a congregation of people.

- Get to know everyone in the congregation. Especially the old people, the widows and the kids. Find the person who seems to have no friends and become his/her friend.

- Practice putting the needs of others before your own needs and wants.

- Enjoy all of God's creation and rejoice in it. Be a happy person.

Elders

Bad And Good Shepherds

In Ezekiel 34, God chastises the leaders of his nation Israel by comparing them to bad shepherds. Let's look at their inactions and actions.

They neglected to…

- Strengthen the weak
- Heal the sick
- Treat the injured
- Bring back the strays
- Search for the lost

Instead they…

- Ate curds
- Clothed selves with wool
- Ate the choice animals
- Ruled harshly and brutally

As a result the flock was scattered and ravaged by wolves. God promised to punish the leaders of Israel and take care of the flock personally. He also promised to provide a true shepherd after the lineage of King David who was and is, Jesus Christ.

Jesus is still the chief shepherd of his people but he has ordained minor shepherds over each local flock of Christians. God expects these human shepherds to strengthen the weak, heal the sick, treat the injured, bring back the strays, search for the lost and rule gently and with kindness.

God loves and highly values his flock of people and expects the same from his shepherds.

www.ingramcontent.com/pod-product-compliance
Lightning Source LLC
LaVergne TN
LVHW021121080426
835512LV00030B/3290